Complete Graded Spelling Lists with Spelling and Vocabulary Exercises

Years Three and Four

BRITISH and WORLD
ENGLISH

KIT'S EDUCATIONAL PUBLISHING

Copyright © 2014 Kit's Educational Publishing

All rights reserved.

ISBN-13:

978-1505823509

ISBN-10:

1505823501

CONTENTS

Introduction   v

YEAR THREE   1

Spelling lists 1-10	2
Revision list 1-10	12
Spelling lists 11-20	13
Revision list 11-20	23
Spelling lists 21-30	24
Revision list 21-30	34
Spelling lists 31-40	35
Revision list 31-40	45
Spelling lists 41-50	46
Revision list 41-50	56

YEAR FOUR   57

Spelling lists 1-10	58
Revision list 1-10	68
Spelling lists 11-20	69
Revision list 11-20	79
Spelling lists 21-30	80
Revision list 21-30	90
Spelling lists 31-40	91
Revision list 31-40	101
Spelling lists 41-50	102
Revision list 41-50	112

ANSWERS   113

Complete Graded Spelling Lists with Spelling and Vocabulary Exercises

INTRODUCTION

Speaking a language is an ability that is learnt naturally by children living in society. Writing a language, by contrast, requires determined effort. It does not come naturally, even to those who are surrounded by the written word. It must be actively taught and learned by means of an extended and repetitive process of trial and error. This is particularly so in the case of English, where so many words break the spelling conventions, such as they are. The ability to spell is clearly central to the ability to write a language; it is no less central to the ability to read. The art of reading effortlessly and with enjoyment is closely correlated with the ability to identify a written word quickly and accurately. Once again, this is particularly difficult in English, because of its unruly spelling. It is thus a great advantage, both to a child's writing and to his or her reading, to have acquired the art of spelling.

As with anything that must be learned by trial and error, it helps to have resources to make the learning process systematic. The spelling and exercise books in the *Complete Graded Spelling Lists* series are intended as such a resource. They are intended as a basic tool in the teaching and testing of spelling to a child. They may also be helpful to those learning or perfecting English later in life and/or as a second language.

How is spelling best taught to a child? Any method of teaching must somehow accommodate the fact that so large a percentage of English words are irregular. Even the most basic 'rules' of English admit of exceptions - and this is particularly true of the simple and high frequency words that children must first master. Rather than teaching by way of rules and their exceptions, many educators now prefer to focus on 'common patterns' of spelling. Following this trend, these word lists are designed to reinforce the associations between words. Words are chosen for their relations to others on the list: the common pattern they share. A successful teaching strategy will exploit this fact, encouraging the child to recognize the connections between the listed words. Once the connections have been identified, any irregularities will appear in sharper focus.

The words of the *Complete Graded Spelling List* books are thus ordered in spelling groups, which follow the developmental stages of learning: from simple short and long vowel sounds (*pan, pane*), through blended and doubled consonants (*brand, barrow*), unstressed syllables and less common phonetic patterns (mirr*or*, mono*logue*) and on to compounded prefixes and suffixes (*appropriate, representation*). The ordering principle for the words of a list is generally alphabetic, using the first and/or last letters of the word and/or the word's primary phonetic element. The extra words in each week are either less common words which follow the same spelling pattern or words which build on the listed words, principally by the addition of prefixes and/or suffixes. These extra words thus help to teach further spelling patterns and show how words within a word family are related (*festive/festival/festivity*, etc.). The spelling of the words in this series follows that of the *Oxford English Dictionary*.

The exercise books in this series - *Complete Graded Spelling Lists with Spelling and Vocabulary Exercises* - provide exercises for your child to work through independently, using these spelling lists. Through a varied range of exercises - matching words to meanings, adding prefixes and suffixes, changing grammatical form, distinguishing homophones and homonyms, and so on - these books extend the educational value of the spelling lists by teaching vocabulary and grammar.

Complete Graded Spelling Lists with Spelling and Vocabulary Exercises

The aim of these exercise books is three-fold:
- first, to increase the child's familiarity with the spelling of the listed words by repeatedly sorting through the list, seeking the answers to various word puzzles;
- second, to reveal the meaning of the listed words, by way of definitions, synonyms, antonyms and other clues;
- and third, to teach the role of grammar in building common spelling patterns. The exercises show how prefixes and suffixes may be added to a root to form grammatical word groups - so, for example, how ~*tion*, ~*al* and ~*ly* are commonly used to make nouns, adjectives and adverbs, respectively.

While simple in format, the exercises are designed to challenge. They are designed to show the underlying patterns of the English language. With practice, these patterns will start to become familiar; in time, they will become commonplace.

While your child can work through these books independently, a parent's help is certainly beneficial. How is this help best given? Encourage your child to focus on the words, asking: why is a given word spelled the way it is? What function does a particular letter (such as the *e* in *page* or the *u* in *plague*) play in the word? Which other words follow the same spelling pattern? Does the word belong to a word family and, if so, what is its root? How do you make this word into a noun, a verb, an adjective or an adverb, as the case may be? Is there another word with the same or similar meaning? Does the word have an opposite? Encourage your child to have favourite words and to use these words in speech and in writing.

In the final upshot, any method of teaching spelling will inevitably involve a great deal of repetition. The most difficult part of teaching spelling is surely to make what is essentially a repetitive task engaging and enjoyable. The fundamental activities here are the simplest of all: writing the word repeatedly, saying it out loud while writing it, and then testing, repeatedly, to reinforce what has been learnt. Identify the words that your child has trouble with and ask your child to write them on sticky notes - or with crayon on a garden path, or on the top of cupcakes using a piping bag, or wherever.

To these fundamental writing activities, add others that are tailored to your own child and his or her interests. Games are a good learning tool. For example, make a jigsaw puzzle of the words your child has trouble with. Write the words on squares of paper, then cut the squares in half or in thirds to separate the letters. The puzzle is then to reconstruct the entire group of words. Or, ask your child to spell a word out loud, but backwards. To do this, he or she will find themselves spelling the word forwards, several times over.

The final piece of advice to any parent teaching spelling to a child is simply to persevere and have patience. Your aim is not simply to teach the several thousand words that your child needs to do well at school. Your aim is to instil a love of words that will stay with your child for life. It is one of the most marvellous of gifts you can give to your child, but it does take time and effort in the giving.

Complete Graded Spelling Lists with Spelling and Vocabulary Exercises

YEAR THREE

List 1	Words with *ar* or *er*
List 2	Words ending in ~*e*
Lists 3-5	Words with *ea*
Lists 6-10	Words starting and ending with two consonants
List 11	More words with *ea*
List 12	Words with *ea* or *oa*
List 13	Words with *oa*
List 14	Words with *ai*
List 15	Words with *ai* or *oi*
Lists 16-18	Words ending in ~*ge*
List 19	Words with *z*
List 20	Words starting with *qu*~
Lists 21-22	Words starting with three consonants
List 23	Words starting or ending with three consonants
Lists 24-25	Words ending in ~*ch*
Lists 26-31	Words with double middle consonants
List 32	Words with *ie*
Lists 33-35	Words with *ou*
List 36	Words with *au*
List 37	Words with double vowel sounds
Lists 38-40	Words ending in ~*le*
Lists 41-44	Words ending in ~*y*
Lists 45-49	Words ending in ~*er*
List 50	Common compound words

Complete Graded Spelling Lists with Spelling and Vocabulary Exercises

YEAR 3 LIST 1

- scar
- star
- scarf
- snarl
- spark
- stark
- smart
- start
- sparse
- carve
- starve
- terse
- verse
- nerve
- serve
- swerve

EXTRA WORDS

- spar
- scarring
- starring
- starving
- swerving

1. Add ~arve or ~erve to make a List 1 word:

- n ~ nerve
- c ~ carve
- s ~ serve
- st ~ starve
- sw ~ swerve

2. Find the List 1 word related to:

- smarter — smart
- swerving — swerve
- sparkler — spark
- sparsely — sparse
- servery — serve
- nervous — nerve

3. Match the List 1 word to its opposite:

- stop or start
- stupid or smart
- dense or sparse
- to feast or to starve
- to command or to serve

4. Match the words to their meaning:

~~terse sparse snarl nerve swerve stark~~

- clear, obvious, glaring — stark
- speaking little, unfriendly — terse
- an angry growl — snarl
- sudden change of direction — swerve
- a type of cell in the body — nerve
- thin, bare, meagre — sparse

2

Complete Graded Spelling Lists with Spelling and Vocabulary Exercises

3. Add ~aste or ~ense to make a List 2 word:

h ~ aste
s ~ ense
d ~ ense
b ~ aste
p ~ aste

1. Find the List 2 word related to:

hasty — haste
half — halve
tension — tense
sensation — sense
density — dense
distasteful — taste

2. Find the List 2 word with the same letters as:

REINS — RINSE
BEATS — BASTE
LOVES — SOLVE
STATE — TASTE

4. Choose the correct word:

sense / cents

I spent ten cents on the lollipop.
He did not have the sense to say no.

tense / tents

There was a tense mood in the room.
The tents in the park were blown over.

waste / waist
waste - rubbish
waist - midriff

The belt will not go round my waist.
I don't want to waste your time.
The food ended up going to waist.

YEAR 3 LIST 2

dense
sense
tense
rinse
else
false
pulse
baste
haste
paste
taste
waste
halve
delve
shelve
solve

EXTRA WORDS

valve
hasty
tasty
halving
shelving

Complete Graded Spelling Lists with Spelling and Vocabulary Exercises

YEAR 3 LIST 3

steal
cream
dream
gleam
steam
clean
jeans
clear
smear
spear
peace
cease
lease
crease
grease
please

EXTRA WORDS

creasing
greasy
cleared
dreamt
peaceful

1. Add ~*eam* or ~*ease* to make a List 3 word:

gl ~ _eam_
gr ~ _ease_
st ~ _eam_
pl ~ _ease_
dr ~ _eam_

2. Match the words to their meaning:

~~gleam cease lease grease smear~~

to shine _gleam_
to stop _cease_
a thick oily substance _grease_
a housing contract _lease_
to smudge or mark _smear_

3. Choose the correct word:

steal / steel
steal - to take
steel - a metal

The sword was made of the strongest _steel_
Who would _steal_ some old shoes?

4. Match the List 3 word to its opposite:

peace or war
clean or dirty
clear or blocked
please or thank you

5. Look at these words:

lease + ~*ed* = leased
lease + ~*ing* = leasing

Now try these:

cease + ~*ed* = _ceased_
cease + ~*ing* = _ceasing_
grease + ~*ed* = _greased_
grease + ~*ing* = _greasing_
please + ~*ed* = _pleased_
please + ~*ing* = _pleasing_

Complete Graded Spelling Lists with Spelling and Vocabulary Exercises

YEAR 3 LIST 4

bleak
sneak
speak
creak
freak
tweak
bleat
pleat
treat
east
beast
feast
least
yeast
heath
sheath

3. Add ~eak or ~east to make a List 4 word:

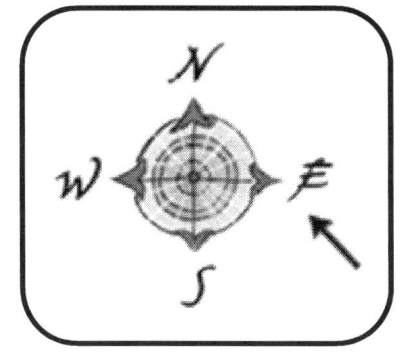

f ~ _east_
fr ~ _eak_
sn ~ _eak_
y ~ _east_
bl ~ _east_

1. Match the List 4 word to its opposite:

most or _least_
famine or _feast_
beauty or _freak_
east or west
trick or _treat_

4. Find the List 4 word related to:

less _least_
spoken _speak_
freaky _freak_
easterly _east_
unsheathed _sheath_

2. Choose the correct word:

creak / creek
creek - a small stream
creak - a small sound

The walls of this house _creak_
We swam in the _creek_ all day.

cheap / cheep
cheap - not expensive
cheep - a bird's sound

The books are _cheap_
I heard a little _cheep_ from the nest.

5. Place the correct word in the sentence:

steal stealing stole
stolen stealth
stealthy stealthily

He is _stealing_ apples from their tree.
She has _stolen_ all my pins.
I _stole_ your pencil by mistake.

EXTRA WORDS

pleated
speaker
creaky
eastern
beastly

Complete Graded Spelling Lists with Spelling and Vocabulary Exercises

YEAR 3 LIST 5

dead
head
bread
dread
deaf
sweat
leant
meant
breast
death
breath
breadth
leave
weave
breathe
beard

EXTRA WORDS

ahead
instead
heave
weaving
breathing

1. Complete the table of verbs:

Present	Past
weave	wove
breathe	breathed
mean	_meant_
lean	_leant_

2. Add the List 5 word that fits best:

life or _death_
stay or _leave_
alive or _dead_
length and _breadth_
bread and butter
as _deaf_ as a post

3. Word maths:

deaf + ~en = _deafen_
deaf + ~en + ~ing = _deafening_
dead + ~en = _deaden_
dead + ~en + ~ing = _deadening_

beard (labelled on picture)

4. Find two List 5 words related to:

deadly _dead_ / _death_
breathing _breathe_ / _breath_

5. Choose the correct word:

lent / leant
lent - past of *loan*
leant - past of *lean*
She _leant_ over and pinched my nose.
I've _lent_ my pen to the teacher.

bred / bread
bred - past of *breed*
bread - a basic food
They've _bred_ the cats to have no tails.
We ate _bread_ and cheese for lunch.

Complete Graded Spelling Lists with Spelling and Vocabulary Exercises

YEAR 3 LIST 6

slang
blank
flank
plank
crank
drank
stank
clamp
cramp
tramp
stamp
blink
clink
brink
drink
stink

3. Add the List 6 noun that fits best:

a _blank_ page
a _plank_ of wood
a _drink_ of tea
a _blink_ of an eye
a _cramp_ in your leg

1. Find two List 6 words related to:

stunk — _stink_, _stank_
drunk — _drank_, _drink_

4. Find the List 6 words with two meanings:

stamp your feet to get off the snow.
- and -
I need a _stamp_ for this letter.

2. Match the word to its meaning:

crank clamp flank brink clink slang

side of an animal — _flank_
a handle on an engine — _crank_
a ringing sound — _clink_
an edge or rim — _brink_
informal words — _slang_
to fasten in place — _clamp_

5. Change one letter of each word to make a List 6 word:

stump — _stamp_
slant — _slang_
crane — _crank_
clump — _clamp_
stand — _stank_

EXTRA WORDS

prank
slink
blankly
stamped
blinker

7

Complete Graded Spelling Lists with Spelling and Vocabulary Exercises

YEAR 3 LIST 7

gland
brand
grand
stand
scalp
brisk
crisp
twist
clung
flung
slung
stung
swung
skunk
drunk
trunk

EXTRA WORDS

slunk
bland
grander
grandest
grandly

---

1. Place the correct word in the sentence:

~~grand~~ ~~grander~~
~~grandest~~ ~~grandly~~
grandeur

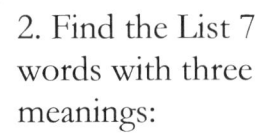

It is the _grandest_ house in the village.
She walked _grandly_ down the aisle.
I am amazed at how _grand_ the ship is.
The _grandeur_ of the house was striking.

2. Find the List 7 words with three meanings:

I cannot _stand_ his rudeness.
- and -
Put your coat on the _stand_ in the hall.
- and -
We were told to _stand_ well back.

* * *

The squirrel lives in the tree's _trunk_.
- and -
The elephant lifted a log with its _trunk_.
- and -
He packed his things in an old _trunk_.

3. Add ~and or ~ung to make a List 7 word:

sl ~ _ung_
cl ~ _ung_
br ~ _and_
gr ~ _and_
fl ~ _ung_
gl ~ _and_

4. Complete the table of verbs:

Present	Past
cling	clung
swing	swung
fling	slung
sling	swung
stand	stood
twist	twisted

Complete Graded Spelling Lists with Spelling and Vocabulary Exercises

YEAR 3 LIST 8

bring
cling
fling
sling
sting
swing
crimp
scold
blond
frond
frost
blunt
grunt
stunt
crust
trust

EXTRA WORDS

skimp
prong
frosty
frostier
frostiest

1. Add the List 8 word that fits best:

a bee _sting_

the early morning _frost_

to have your arm in a _sling_

to _cling_ to a life raft

the _frond_ of a palm tree

to dye your hair _blond_

2. Complete the table of verbs:

Present	Past
sting	stung
trust	trusted
sling	flung
bring	brought

3. Add ~ing or ~ust to make a List 8 word:

tr ~ _ust_
st ~ _ing_
fl ~ _ing_
cr ~ _ust_
cl ~ _ing_
sw ~ _ing_

4. Match the word to its meaning:

crimp frond prong scold stunt blunt

not sharp _blunt_

to criticize in a nagging way _scold_

a long leaf _frond_

a pointed end of something, that juts out _prong_

a feat, a clever act _stunt_

to make tight curls _crimp_

Complete Graded Spelling Lists with Spelling and Vocabulary Exercises

YEAR 3 LIST 9

blend
spend
trend
spent
smelt
dwelt
crept
slept
swept
crest
clump
plump
slump
stump
spasm
prism

EXTRA WORDS

trump
frisk
crispy
crispier
crispiest

1. Add ~*end* or ~*ump* to make a List 9 word:

st ~ _ump_
bl ~ _end_
sl ~ _ump_
sp ~ _end_
pl ~ _ump_

2. Complete the table of verbs:

Present	Past
creep	crept
spend	spent
sweep	swept
dwell	dwelt
sleep	slept
slump	slumped

3. Find the List 9 word with two meanings:

The army thundered over the _crest_ of the hill.
- and -
The parrot has a fine _crest_ of feathers.

4. Place the correct word in the sentence:

sleep slept sleepy
sleeping ~~sleepier~~
~~sleepless~~ sleepiness
sleepily sleeplessness

I felt _sleepier_ than I ever had before.
We had a _sleepless_ night, worrying about where he was.
She sat _sleepy_ watching the movie.

5. Add the List 9 noun that fits best:

a tree _stump_
a fashion _trend_
a _spasm_ of pain
a _clump_ of grass
a _prism_ of light
a _blend_ of coffee beans

Complete Graded Spelling Lists with Spelling and Vocabulary Exercises

YEAR 3 LIST 10

**flask
clasp
grasp
craft
grant
plant
slant
blast
blind
drift
swift
spilt
stilt
flint
glint
print**

1. Add ~*ant* or ~*int* to make a List 10 word:

pr ~ _int_
pl ~ _ant_
fl ~ _int_
gl ~ _int_
sl ~ _ant_
gr ~ _ant_

---

2. Add the List 10 noun that fits best:

a _flask_ of water
a _plant_ in a pot
a _blast_ of cold air
the _print_ of a newspaper
the _clasp_ of a bracelet
the _glint_ of a diamond

---

3. Match the word to its meaning:

~~slant~~ ~~glint~~ ~~flask~~
~~grant~~ ~~clasp~~ ~~flint~~

to give or to allow _grant_

a container for liquid _flask_

a sharp grey stone _glint_ ~~slant~~

to lean or tilt _slant_

to reflect light _glint_

to hold tightly _clasp_

---

4. Find the List 10 words with two meanings:

She was new to the _craft_ of weaving.
- and -
At dawn, the fishing _craft_ head home.

* * *

Don't forget to water the _plant_.
- and -
The power _plant_ is outside the town.

EXTRA WORDS

**graft
grind
stint
planted
glinted**

11

YEAR 3   WEEKS 1-10
50 Word Revision List

bread	dwelt	breath
trust	scold	rinse
leave	least	sheath
plump	cramp	cease
peace	beard	treat
stump	scalp	jeans
head	blink	verse
glint	waste	haste
meant	sneak	smear
crust	plant	blond
swung	death	feast
swift	spasm	swerve
blunt	please	carve
spear	scarf	halve
flank	dream	swing
swept	shelve	creak
starve		craft

Complete Graded Spelling Lists with Spelling and Vocabulary Exercises

3. Find the List 11 word related to:

readiness _ready_
stealthily _stealth_
threatened _threat_
unsteadily _steady_
torn _tear_
worn _wear_

YEAR 3
LIST 11

bear
pear
tear
wear
swear
health
wealth
stealth
tread
thread
threat
realm
ready
steady
heavy
heart

1. Add the List 11 word that fits best:

ready, set, go
heavy or light
sickness or _health_
poverty or _wealth_
needle and _thread_
the beat of your _heart_
to _swear_ an oath
to _wear_ our your clothes

4. Choose the correct word:

wear / where
I don't know _where_ my jacket is.
I'll _wear_ my new cap today.

bear / bare
bear - an animal
bare - not covered
I was cold because my arms were _bare_.
The _bear_ at the zoo does tricks.

pear / pair
pear - a fruit
pair - a twosome
I made a _pear_ tart for dessert.
I don't have a spare _pair_ of shoes.

2. Find the List 11 word that can be spoken in two ways:

A single _tear_ fell down his cheek.
- and -
I'm trying not to _tear_ the paper.

EXTRA WORDS

cleanse
hearth
readily
steadily
heavily

YEAR 3 LIST 12

- earl
- early
- earn
- heard
- pearl
- learn
- yearn
- earth
- search
- break
- steak
- great
- board
- broad
- coarse
- hoarse

EXTRA WORDS

- dearth
- hoard
- learnt
- earlier
- earliest

1. Add *ea* or *ear* to make a List 12 word:

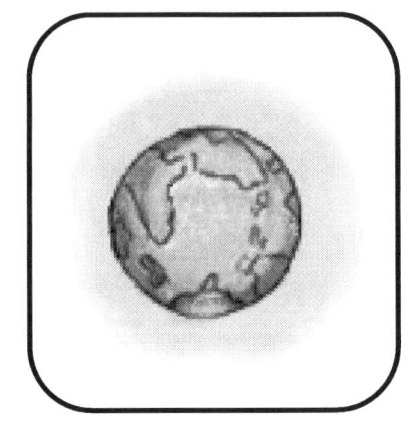

br ~ k __ea__
s ~ ch __ear__
~ th __ear__
p ~ l __ear__
gr ~ t __ea__
y ~ n __ear__

2. Match the List 12 word to its opposite:

__great__ or small
__early__ or late
__coarse__ or smooth
__broad__ or narrow
__heard__ or misheard

3. Add the List 12 word that sounds the same as:

urn __earn__
brake __break__
grate __great__
bored __board__
herd __heard__
horse __hoarse__
course __coarse__

4. Choose the correct word:

board - a thick sheet   **bored** - tired, uninterested
I was __bored__ with the book I was reading.
We looked for our names on the __board__

grate - to scratch against   **great** - large or good
It is such a __great__ movie, I want to see it again.
The noise tends to __grate__ on my ears.

Complete Graded Spelling Lists with Spelling and Vocabulary Exercises

YEAR 3 LIST 13

coal
foal
goal
oath
cloak
croak
groan
float
gloat
throat
coach
poach
boast
coast
roast
toast

3. Add ~oat or ~oast to make a List 13 word:

r ~ _____
gl ~ _____
t ~ _____
thr ~ _____
fl ~ _____

1. Match the word to its meaning:

**croak foal oath
poach gloat coal**

a solemn promise
_____

to steal something
_____

a young horse
_____

a deep, hoarse sound
_____

to be too pleased with yourself _____

a black rock, used as fuel
_____

4. Word maths:

croak + ~ing = _____

cloak + ~ed = _____

toast + ~er = _____

coast + ~al = _____

goal + ~less = _____

boast + ~full = _____

throat + ~y + ~est = _____

2. Choose the correct word:

groan / grown
groan - a moan
grown - past of *grow*

She gave a _____ when she saw me.
You have _____ so tall lately.

5. Find the List 13 word with two meanings:

I let my bike _____ to the finish line.
- and -
We took the road along the _____.

EXTRA WORDS

goad
coax
hoax
coaches
poaches

Complete Graded Spelling Lists with Spelling and Vocabulary Exercises

YEAR 3 LIST 14

bail
wail
vain
braid
snail
frail
trail
claim
plain
brain
drain
grain
stain
train
flair
stairs

EXTRA WORDS

staid
flail
brail
slain
plait

1. Find the List 14 word that rhymes with:

cares　_____
bear　_____
made　_____
same　_____

2. Choose the correct word:

wail / whale
wail - a cry
whale - sea animal

The cat's _____ can be heard from afar.
The _____ sprung up out of the water.

plane / plain
plane - a flat surface
plain - ordinary, obvious

She wore a _____ blue dress to the party.
The _____ was covered in lush grass.

stairs / stares
stairs - steps
stares - looks, glares

I fell on the _____ up to the stage.
She sits and _____ into the distance.

3. Add ~ail or ~ain to make a List 14 word:

sn ~　_____
st ~　_____
dr ~　_____
v ~　_____
fr ~　_____
pl ~　_____

4. Find the List 14 word related to:

frailty　_____
proclaim　_____
drainage　_____
granary　_____
vanity　_____
bailiff　_____

Complete Graded Spelling Lists with Spelling and Vocabulary Exercises

YEAR 3 LIST 15

trait
faint
paint
saint
waist
faith
raise
praise
joint
point
hoist
moist
spoil
voice
noise
choice

EXTRA WORDS

gait
taint
oink
poise
foist

3. Add *ai* or *oi* to make a List 15 word:

sp ~ l _____
w ~ st _____
tr ~ t _____
m ~ st _____
h ~ st _____
f ~ th _____

4. Match the word to its meaning:

moist saint waist
hoist spoil trait

to lift up _____
ruin _____
holy person _____
attribute _____
midriff _____
wet _____

1. Match the List 15 word to its opposite:

_____ or sinner
_____ or dry
_____ or silence
_____ or blame

2. Choose the correct word:

waist / waste

The dress has a sash at the _____.
It is a _____ to throw out the food.

prays / praise

You must _____ him for his good work.
She _____ every day at church.

5. Find the List 15 word with two meanings:

to grow dizzy and collapse _____
- and -
weak, pale, not dark _____

YEAR 3 LIST 16

stage
barge
large
charge
badge
cadge
range
change
orange
budge
fudge
judge
nudge
smudge
grudge
trudge

EXTRA WORDS

budge
sludge
barged
ranged
begrudged

---

1. Add ~*arge* or ~*udge* to make a List 16 word:

ch ~ _____
gr ~ _____
l ~ _____
sm ~ _____
j ~ _____
n ~ _____

---

2. Find the List 16 words with two meanings:

It was the final _____ of the race.
- *and* -
I had never acted on _____ before.

* * *

The bull will _____ if you go near.
- *and* -
There is a _____ for using the printer.

* * *

He took a _____ of clothes to school.
- *and* -
I have no _____ left in my pocket.

---

3. Find the List 16 word from the clue:

_____ or small
_____ and jury
_____ and lemon
to eat _____

---

4. Match the word to its meaning:

**cadge budge grudge
nudge smudge trudge**

to smear _____
a resentful feeling
_____
to move, shift
_____
to ask for something from someone
_____
to prod or bump
_____
to walk wearily
_____

YEAR 3 LIST 17

**urge
purge
surge
bulge
ridge
bridge
fridge
binge
hinge
singe
cringe
fringe
twinge
lunge
plunge
lounge**

EXTRA WORDS

**tinge
midge
surging
bridging
plunging**

1. Add ~*idge* or ~*inge* to make a List 17 word:

   cr ~ _____
   tw ~ _____
   r ~ _____
   b ~ _____
   br ~ _____

2. Write these words in alphabetical order:

   twinge purge lounge ridge lunge singe

   _____
   _____
   _____
   _____
   _____
   _____

3. Look at these words:

   urge + ~*ed* = urged
   urge + ~*ing* = urging

   Now try these:

   singe + ~*ed* = _____

   lunge + ~*ed* = _____

   lounge + ~*ing* = _____

   bridge + ~*ing* = _____

   surge + ~*ing* = _____

4. Find the List 17 word from the clue:

   goes across a river: _____

   where you sit to relax: _____

   a short, sharp feeling: _____

   on the side of a door: _____

   to burn slightly: _____

   a swelling or lump: _____

YEAR 3 LIST 18

merge
verge
forge
gorge
edge
hedge
ledge
wedge
pledge
sledge
dredge
dodge
lodge
sponge
scourge
stodge

EXTRA WORDS

dirge
gauge
merging
edging
lodging

1. Find the List 18 words with two meanings:

The popcorn tends to _____ itself in your teeth.
 - and -
We stayed at an old hunting _____.

* * *

We walked through the _____ to the waterfall.
 - and -
He likes to _____ himself on sweets.

2. Word maths:

sponge + ~y = _____

pledge + ~ing = _____

lodge + ~er = _____

forge + ~er + ~y = _____

dis~ + lodge + ~ed = _____

di~ + verge + ~ent = _____

e~ + merge + ~ing = _____

3. Add ~edge or ~orge to make a List 18 word:

l ~ _____
f ~ _____
w ~ _____
h ~ _____
g ~ _____

4. Match the word to its meaning:

dodge wedge pledge scourge dredge verge

edge, rim _____
a promise _____
to bring to the surface _____
a thin slice of something _____
a thing causing damage _____
to move quickly to miss something _____

Complete Graded Spelling Lists with Spelling and Vocabulary Exercises

YEAR 3 LIST 19

daze
faze
gaze
haze
laze
maze
raze
size
doze
blaze
glaze
craze
froze
prize
jazz
buzz

2. Add ~*aze* or ~*oze* to make a List 19 word:

bl ~ _____
fr ~ _____
cr ~ _____
m ~ _____

1. Choose the correct word:

days / daze
days - plural of *day*
daze - confusion

He was in a _____ after her performance.
The _____ go past so quickly.

lays / laze
laze - rest sleepily
lays - from verb *to lie*

She _____ the table for dinner carefully.
They will _____ all day, doing nothing.

dose / doze
dose - a measure
doze - to take a nap

The dog likes to _____ in the sun.
I must take a _____ of medicine every night.

pries / prize
pries - from verb *to pry*
prize - an award

He _____ into other people's business.
He won the _____ for good work.

3. Match the word to its meaning:

blaze raze faze
haze craze glaze

a large fire _____
a thin, glossy coating _____
a fine cloud _____
a fashion _____
to destroy completely _____
to disturb or upset _____

4. Look at these:

laze + ~*y* = lazy
buzz + ~*y* = buzzy

Now try these:

doze + ~*y* = _____
haze + ~*y* = _____
craze + ~*y* = _____
jazz + ~*y* = _____

EXTRA WORDS

graze
hazy
dozy
lazily
crazily

YEAR 3 LIST 20

quay
qualm
quash
quake
quail
quaint
quell
quest
quench
quite
quiet
quill
quilt
quote
quota
quoit

EXTRA WORDS

quotas
quenches
quaking
quelling
quoting

1. Match the word to its meaning:

qualm quest quota
quash quell quail

to put down with force _____

the amount of something allowed _____

long journey to find something _____

to set aside _____

a nagging worry _____

to show fear _____

2. Add the List 20 word that fits best:

_____ as a mouse

an earth _____

a _____ on a bed

to _____ your thirst

to _____ a riot

to throw a _____

a _____ to kill a dragon

3. Find the List 20 word that rhymes with:

messed _____
right _____
stale _____
break _____
arm _____
wash _____
boat _____

4. Find the List 20 word with two meanings:

the sharp spine of a porcupine
_____
- and -
a long feather, used for writing
_____

YEAR 3   WEEKS 11-20
50 Word Revision List

braid	threat	pearl
jazz	moist	urge
oath	wear	froze
praise	judge	roast
search	dodge	quiet
ledge	coach	raise
noise	doze	gorge
quench	waist	steady
quaint	break	voice
lounge	prize	fridge
wealth	board	blaze
orange	realm	learn
plunge	brain	saint
change	croak	quota
float	heart	sponge
quay	stairs	flair
maze		toast

YEAR 3 LIST 21

splash
split
splint
strap
straw
stray
strain
strange
street
strip
stride
strike
stripe
strive
stroll
stroke

EXTRA WORDS

splice
strobe
strapped
stripped
striped

1. Look at these:

nap + ~*ing* = napping
nail + ~*ing* = nailing
note + ~*ing* = noting

Now try these:

stride + ~*ing* = _____

split + ~*ing* = _____

stroke + ~*ing* = _____

strain + ~*ing* = _____

strap + ~*ing* = _____

strive + ~*ing* = _____

2. Find the List 21 word that rhymes with:

eyed _____
door _____
pane _____
bowl _____
oak _____
they _____

3. Write these words in alphabetical order:

splint strip stroll
strike split stripe

_____
_____
_____
_____
_____
_____

4. Add the List 20 word that fits best:

a _____ dog
a _____ sign
the final _____
a _____ of good luck

24

Complete Graded Spelling Lists with Spelling and Vocabulary Exercises

YEAR 3 LIST 22

scrap
scrape
scrawl
script
screw
screen
scream
scroll
scrub
scrum
spray
spree
sprig
sprain
spread
sprout

EXTRA WORDS

sprawl
sprite
spruce
scrapped
scraped

---

3. Add *scr~* or *spr~* to make a List 22 word:

~ ead _____
~ out _____
~ ew _____
~ um _____
~ oll _____
~ ay _____

1. Add the List 22 word that fits best:

a cork _____
a fire _____
a _____ of water
a small _____ of flowers
a tiny _____ of paper

4. Find the List 22 word that rhymes with:

bed _____
key _____
true _____
mane _____
mean _____
theme _____

2. Place the correct word in the sentence:

script scripture scripted unscripted scriptural prescription

The _____ is a set of holy books. Have you read the play's _____? The doctor gave me a _____ for some medicine.

5. Find the List 22 word with two meanings:

I had to _____ to get the paint off.
- and -
A bushy _____ covered the land.

YEAR 3 LIST 23

strait
stream
streak
stress
stretch
string
strong
struck
strength
length
batch
catch
fetch
itch
ditch
notch

EXTRA WORDS

strut
strung
lengthen
strengthen
strengthened

---

1. Find the List 23 word rhyming with:

week _____
guess _____
mate _____
theme _____

2. Place the correct word in the sentence:

**strong strongly
stronger strongest
strength strengthen
strengthening**

He does not know his own _____.
You must _____ your muscles.
She is the _____ girl I know.
I _____ advise you to say sorry.

3. Find the List 23 word with two meanings:

She will try to _____ you along with excuses.
- and -
I need _____ to tie the balloons.

4. Find the List 23 word closest in meaning to:

trauma _____
hit _____
river _____
trench _____
span _____
carry _____

5. Write these words in alphabetical order:

**stretch itch strength
notch length fetch**

_____
_____
_____
_____
_____
_____

Complete Graded Spelling Lists with Spelling and Vocabulary Exercises

YEAR 3 LIST 24

hatch
latch
match
patch
thatch
snatch
scratch
sketch
hitch
pitch
witch
stitch
switch
hutch
clutch
crutch

3. Add ~*atch* or ~*itch* to make a List 24 word:

scr ~ _____
th ~ _____
st ~ _____
sn ~ _____
sw ~ _____

1. Find the List 24 word closest in meaning to:

grasp _____
grab _____
swap _____
contest _____
sew _____

4. Find the List 24 words with two meanings:

I struck a _____ to light the candle.
- and -
The blue shoes don't _____ the dress.
* * *
He lifted the _____ to the cabin below.
- and -
The eggs will _____ in about a week.

2. Add the List 24 verb that fits best:

to _____ the door
to _____ an itch
to _____ a roof
to _____ a seam
to _____ a tent
to _____ a diagram

5. Add the correct word:

which / witch

_____ cake would you prefer? She enjoyed acting the role of _____.

EXTRA WORDS

retch
twitch
blotchy
scratchy
sketchy

YEAR 3 LIST 25

belch
bench
clench
drench
trench
inch
finch
pinch
winch
flinch
bunch
hunch
lunch
munch
punch
crunch

EXTRA WORDS

mulch
stench
clinch
trenches
pinches

1. Match the word to its meaning:

**clench winch
flinch hunch
trench drench**

to soak with water
_____

to hold tightly together _____

a vague guess or suspicion
_____

a long, narrow ditch
_____

to pull back suddenly
_____

to lift or pull, using a rope
_____

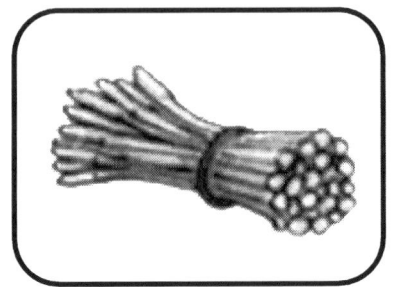

2. Add the List 25 word that fits best:

a _____ of flowers

a _____ of salt

to _____ your fist

to eat your _____

to dig a _____

to sit on a _____

3. Add ~*ench* or ~*unch* to make a List 25 word:

p ~ _____
dr ~ _____
cr ~ _____
cl ~ _____
tr ~ _____

4. Look at these:

inch + ~*s* = inch<u>es</u>
trench + ~*s* = trench<u>es</u>

Now try these:

crunch + ~*s* = _____

finch + ~*s* = _____

hunch + ~*s* = _____

bench + ~*s* = _____

belch + ~*s* = _____

Complete Graded Spelling Lists with Spelling and Vocabulary Exercises

YEAR 3 LIST 26

batter
latter
matter
chatter
shatter
scatter
clatter
flatter
platter
splatter
better
letter
bitter
litter
glitter
twitter

EXTRA WORDS

patter
spatter
fritter
chattered
flattered

Mrs Daisy Belmonte,
15 Cowslip Drive,
Ontario,
Canada
ON L5N 6X6

---

1. Add ~atter or ~itter to make a List 26 word:

gl ~ _____
sc ~ _____
spl ~ _____
tw ~ _____
cl ~ _____

---

2. Look at these:

chatter + ~ed = chattered
chatter + ~ing = chattering

Now try these:

shatter + ~ed = _____

litter + ~ing = _____

splatter + ~ed = _____

batter + ~ing = _____

---

3. Find the List 26 words with two meanings:

The wind tends to _____ the houses.
- and -
The _____ is ready to cook.

* * *

I will take the _____ to the post office.
- and -
What is the last _____ of your name?

* * *

What is the _____ with your eye?
- and -
Take a small piece of plant _____ and put it under the microscope.

---

4. Add the List 26 word that fits best:

_____ or worse
former or _____
sweet or _____
_____ in the bin
_____ in the post
to _____ like glass
to _____ like a bird

YEAR 3 LIST 27

robber
rubber
blubber
adder
udder
rudder
shudder
utter
butter
gutter
mutter
clutter
flutter
shutter
stutter
splutter

EXTRA WORDS

slobber
fodder
uttered
robbery
rubbery

---

1. Match the word to its meaning:

stutter splutter udder rudder clutter shudder

the teats of a cow _____

a spitting or choking noise _____

the lever on a boat which controls its direction _____

to stumble on words while talking _____

to tremble or shake _____

a muddle of disorderly things _____

---

2. Add the List 27 word that fits best:

bread and _____

pencil and _____

a boat's _____

a cow's _____

a _____ of wings

the _____ on a roof

the _____ on a window

---

3. Add ~*ubber* or ~*utter* to make a List 27 word:

bl ~ _____
st ~ _____
fl ~ _____
r ~ _____
sh ~ _____

---

4. Find the List 27 words with two meanings:

He didn't _____ a single word to me.
- *and* -
It was an _____ waste of time.

* * *

The child started to _____ and wail.
- *and* -
The fat of whales is called _____.

Complete Graded Spelling Lists with Spelling and Vocabulary Exercises

YEAR 3 LIST 28

offer
differ
suffer
hammer
stammer
inner
banner
manner
dinner
pepper
zipper
flipper
slipper
copper
stopper
supper

3. Add ~*nner* or ~*pper* to make a List 28 word:

fli ~ _____
pe ~ _____
ba ~ _____
su ~ _____
ma ~ _____

1. Find the List 28 word related to:

inning _____
dining _____
unstoppable _____
unmannered _____
insufferable _____

4. Look at these:

offer + ~*ed* = offered
offer + ~*ing* = offering

Now try these:

suffer + ~*ed* = _____

suffer + ~*ing* = _____

stammer + ~*ed* = _____

stammer + ~*ing* = _____

2. Place the correct word in the sentence:

**differ differing
differed difference
different differentiate**

The test _____ from the one last week.
There's no _____ between this and that.
She and I _____ in that she is tall.
He looks _____ every time I see him.

5. Add the List 28 noun that fits best:

_____ on a dress
_____ on a foot
_____ on a whale
_____ on a bottle

EXTRA WORDS

coffer
sinner
winner
snapper
shopper

Complete Graded Spelling Lists with Spelling and Vocabulary Exercises

YEAR 3 LIST 29

shallow
bellow
fellow
mellow
yellow
billow
pillow
follow
hollow
arrow
barrow
narrow
sparrow
borrow
sorrow
burrow

EXTRA WORDS

fallow
willow
marrow
barrowful
sorrowful

1. Word maths:

follow + ~ing =
_____

narrow + ~ly =
_____

sorrow + ~full =
_____

borrow + ~er =
_____

shallow + ~est =
_____

2. Find the List 29 word closest in meaning to:

den _____

shout _____

empty _____

sadness _____

chap _____

3. Add the List 29 noun that fits best:

to dig a _____

to wheel a _____

to plump a _____

to shoot an _____

4. Match the List 29 word to its opposite:

happiness or _____

_____ or wide

lend or _____

_____ or deep

lead or _____

5. Place the correct word in the sentence:

sorrow sorrowful sorrowfully sorry sorrier sorriest

He gave us the most _____ look.

His look was full of _____.

He looked at us _____.

32

Complete Graded Spelling Lists with Spelling and Vocabulary Exercises

YEAR 3 LIST 30

sudden
pollen
sullen
happen
kitten
mitten
coffin
muffin
ribbon
common
summon
cotton
button
blossom
bottom
possum

3. Complete these List 30 words:

____ den   ____ bon

____ sum   ____ pen

1. Word maths:

happen + ~*ing* =
_____

summon + ~*ed* =
_____

sudden + ~*ly* =
_____

common + ~*er* =
_____

un~ + button + ~*ed* =
_____

4. Find the List 30 word that means:

shared   _____
beckon   _____
abrupt   _____
brooding _____
band, tie _____
occur   _____

2. Place the correct word in the sentence:

common commoner commonest uncommon commonly uncommonly commonness

Bears are _____ seen in the woods.
It is the _____ type of lawn of all.
It is unusual for a prince to marry a _____.

5. Find the List 30 words with two meanings:

The baby was given an injection on the _____.
- and -
We looked up from the _____ of the hill.

* * *

The tree was covered in pink _____.
- and -
His talent for music did not _____ until he was older.

EXTRA WORDS

barren
smitten
puffin
gallon
mutton

YEAR 3   WEEKS 21-30
50 Word Revision List

witch	strange	mutter
stream	glitter	bunch
utter	ditch	stroll
muffin	spread	clutch
crunch	shallow	summon
cotton	snatch	narrow
sorrow	slipper	shatter
possum	stroke	bottom
sudden	manner	suffer
straw	sketch	screw
rudder	stripe	yellow
offer	splatter	drench
catch	script	scratch
pollen	kitten	stitch
flinch	length	hammer
spray	fetch	borrow
stretch		scream

Complete Graded Spelling Lists with Spelling and Vocabulary Exercises

YEAR 3 LIST 31

channel
flannel
kennel
funnel
tunnel
barrel
vessel
nugget
bullet
plummet
puppet
rabbit
summit
ballot
carrot
parrot

EXTRA WORDS

mussel
fillet
maggot
funnelling
tunnelling

1. 1. Add ~*nnel* or ~*rrot* to make a List 31 word:

fu ~ _____
ca ~ _____
pa ~ _____
tu ~ _____
fla ~ _____

2. Look at these:

tunnel + ~*ed* = tunne**ll**ed
tunnel + ~*ing* = tunne**ll**ing

Now try these:

funnel + ~*ed* = _____

funnel + ~*ing* = _____

channel + ~*ed* = _____

channel + ~*ing* = _____

3. Find the List 31 noun that fits best:

a glove _____
a secret _____
a _____ of gold
a _____ for a gun
a dog's _____
the _____ of a mountain
the paws of a _____

4. Find the List 31 words with two meanings:

Change the _____ on the television.
- *and* -
The rainwater flows down this _____ into the sea.

* * *

They store the wine in a _____ in the cellar.
- *and* -
The children _____ along without looking where they are going.

* * *

The _____ has bright blue feathers.
- *and* -
The girl will _____ whatever you say.

35

YEAR 3 LIST 32

pier
tier
view
brief
chief
grief
thief
field
yield
shield
priest
niece
piece
siege
shriek
friend

EXTRA WORDS

wield
fiend
chiefs
grieves
thieves

---

1. Add ~*ief* or ~*iece* to make a List 32 word:

th ~ _____
n ~ _____
gr ~ _____
p ~ _____
br ~ _____

2. Choose the correct word:

peer / pier
pier - jetty, quay
peer - to look, gaze

I sat on the _____ and looked out to sea. We tried to _____ far into the distance.

tear / tier
tear - from weeping
tier - a level or layer

We sat on the second _____ of the stand. A _____ trickled down his cheek.

peace / piece
peace - not war
piece - a part or section

The puppies give us no _____ at all. Please have a _____ of cake.

3. Add the List 32 word that fits best:

_____ or nephew
_____ or foe
_____ or priestess
_____ or lengthy
a _____ of paper
the _____ of a clan
to fish off a _____

4. Add the same word twice to each sentence, to make a mnemonic:

Will you eat a _____ce of _____?

* * *

There is no _____ to being a fri_____.

Complete Graded Spelling Lists with Spelling and Vocabulary Exercises

YEAR 3 LIST 33

cloud
proud
shroud
bound
found
hound
mound
pound
round
sound
wound
ground
flour
scour
house
mouse

1. Find the List 33 word related to:

mice _____
sonic _____
pride _____

2. Find the List 33 words with two or more meanings:

I paid one _____.
- and -
The drummers like to _____ the drums.

* * *

There were ants all over the _____.
- and -
I _____ the spices in to a fine dust.

* * *

The doctor _____ my foot very tight.
- and -
He leapt over the fence in a single _____.

3. Add ~oud or ~ound to make a List 33 word:

m ~ _____
shr ~ _____
gr ~ _____
pr ~ _____
cl ~ _____
h ~ _____

4. Choose the correct word:

flour / flower
flour - ground grain
flower - on a plant

This cake does not need _____.
The roses should _____ in June.

5. Complete the table of verbs:

Present	Past
find	_____
wind	_____
bind	_____
grind	_____
_____	scoured

EXTRA WORDS

douse
louse
spouse
floury
mousy

YEAR 3 LIST 34

scout
snout
spout
trout
stout
shout
ouch
couch
pouch
crouch
mouth
south
count
mount
joust
blouse

EXTRA WORDS

clout
flout
vouch
grouch
slouch

---

1. Add the List 34 word that fits best:

   north or _____

   slender or _____

   to _____ orders

   to _____ water

   to _____ to ten

   to _____ a horse

   to fish for _____

2. Match the word to its meaning:

   snout joust scout stout crouch pouch

   the front part of an animal's face
   _____

   to fight with lances
   _____

   a bag or purse
   _____

   to squat close to the ground
   _____

   to look for information
   _____

   heavy, solid
   _____

3. Add ~*out* or ~*ouch* to make a List 34 word:

   c ~ _____
   sp ~ _____
   tr ~ _____
   cr ~ _____
   sn ~ _____

4. Find the List 34 words with two or more meanings:

   The _____ lives in a mansion.
   - and -
   I watched her _____ the cash.

   * * *

   Don't talk with your _____ full.
   - and -
   We camped at the river's _____.

YEAR 3 LIST 35

soul
mould
soup
group
wound
youth
court
course
source
ounce
bounce
pounce
young
touch
double
trouble

EXTRA WORDS

mourn
moult
trounce
soulful
youthful

---

3. Word maths:

double + ~ed = _____

bounce + ~er = _____

trouble + ~ing = _____

soul + ~less = _____

re~ + source + ~full = _____

1. Add ~ce or ~se to make a List 35 word:

sour ~ _____
cour ~ _____
poun ~ _____

---

2. Place the words:

soul course group trouble mould youth touch source

words where *ou* sounds like the *u* in *cup* :

_____ _____

words where *ou* sounds like the *oo* in *room* :

_____ _____

words where *ou* sounds like the *or* in *fort* :

_____ _____

words where *ou* sounds like the *ow* in *bowl* :

_____ _____

---

4. Choose the correct word:

sole / soul
sole - only, single
soul - inner self

He puts his heart and _____ into his work.
She was his _____ reason for going.

coarse / course
coarse - not fine
course - path, route

We must follow the _____ of the river.
The fabric is _____ on the skin.

sauce / source
sauce - topping for food
source - origin

They followed the river to its _____.
Would you like some _____ on your chips?

YEAR 3 LIST 36

aunt
haul
maul
faun
taut
sauce
cause
pause
clause
fault
vault
haunt
taunt
flaunt
launch
paunch

EXTRA WORDS

gaunt
saucer
haunches
hauled
mauled

---

1. Add a verb from List 36:

uncle or _____
loose or _____
_____ or effect
deer and _____
pasta with _____
to _____ a rocket

---

2. Choose the correct word:

mall / maul
mall - arcade of shops
maul - bite, claw

There is a new cinema in the _____.
Don't let the dog _____ your shoes.

paws / pause
paws - feet of an animal
pause - short break

She had the dog's _____ on her lap.
She gave a _____ to catch her breath.

hall / haul
hall - corridor
haul - tow or drag

We had to _____ the boat to the lake.
She ran down the _____ to the door.

---

3. Add ~ce or ~se to make a List 36 word:

cau ~ _____
clau ~ _____
sau ~ _____

---

4. Add a List 36 word that sounds like:

aren't _____
taught _____
claws _____

---

5. Find the List 36 word that rhymes with:

horse _____
wart _____
born _____
can't _____

Complete Graded Spelling Lists with Spelling and Vocabulary Exercises

YEAR 3 LIST 37

area
idea
create
liar
duel
fuel
cruel
poem
alien
diet
duet
fluid
ruin
neon
lion
riot

1. Add the List 37 word that fits best:

kind or _____

_____ or lioness

solid or _____

_____ lights

_____ spaceship

to read a _____

to play a _____

2. Find the List 37 word related to:

idealize _____

alienate _____

poetry _____

creativity _____

3. Choose the correct word:

dual / duel
dual - involving two
duel - a fight with weapons

They fought a _____ to the death with their swords.
The machine has _____ functions, to heat and to cool.

liar / lyre
liar - someone who lies
lyre - a musical instrument

She strummed the _____ gently.
He is such a _____, I don't believe him.

4. Add List 37 words to the table:

Noun	Adjective
_____	ruinous
_____	poetic
cruelty	_____
fluidity	_____
_____	riotous
_____	dietary
_____	ideal

EXTRA WORDS

poetry
naive
mosaic
deity
fiord

YEAR 3 LIST 38

babble
scrabble
nibble
scribble
gobble
hobble
wobble
bubble
rubble
baffle
raffle
ruffle
scuffle
giggle
wiggle
goggle

EXTRA WORDS

rabble
dribble
cobble
stubble
haggle

1. Look at these:

   rose + ~y = rosy
   bone + ~y = bony

Now try these:

bubble + ~y = _____

wiggle + ~y = _____

giggle + ~y = _____

wobble + ~y = _____

2. Match the word to its meaning:

   hobble baffle rubble
   babble scuffle ruffle

to puzzle or confuse
_____

piles of broken rock or brick
_____

a short, scrambled movement or fight
_____

senseless talk
_____

to disturb or fluster
_____

to walk with difficulty or a limp
_____

3. Add ~*bble* or ~*ggle* to make a List 38 word:

ho ~ _____
wo ~ _____
wi ~ _____
bu ~ _____
scri ~ _____
gi ~ _____

4. Add the List 38 word that fits best:

to _____ a finger
to _____ your food
to _____ a note
a _____ ticket
a _____ bath
a _____ of voices

Complete Graded Spelling Lists with Spelling and Vocabulary Exercises

YEAR 3 LIST 39

paddle
saddle
middle
riddle
cuddle
huddle
muddle
puddle
battle
cattle
rattle
kettle
nettle
settle
little
bottle

3. Word maths:

settle + ~*er* = _____

huddle + ~*ed* = _____

cuddle + ~*y* = _____

rattle + ~*ing* = _____

1. Add ~*uddle* or ~*ettle* to make a List 39 word:

p ~ _____
s ~ _____
h ~ _____
k ~ _____
c ~ _____

4. Add the List 39 noun that fits best:

to herd _____
to solve a _____
to win a _____
to boil a _____
to shake a _____
to open a _____

2. Find the List 39 words with two meanings:

She rode the horse without a _____.
- and -
He tends to _____ me with his problems.

* * *

The children like to _____ in the pool.
- and -
After dropping the oar, I had only a _____.

5. Place the correct word in the sentence:

settle settler settling unsettling resettled unsettled settlement

A _____ grew up around the lake.
They are _____ in to their new house.
I had an _____ feeling of danger.

EXTRA WORDS

fiddle
griddle
prattle
mettle
throttle

YEAR 3 LIST 40

apple
grapple
ripple
cripple
topple
supple
hassle
tussle
dazzle
sizzle
drizzle
grizzle
nozzle
muzzle
nuzzle
puzzle

EXTRA WORDS

fizzle
guzzle
swizzle
dappled
puzzled

1. Add ~*ssle* or ~*zzle* to make a List 40 word:

gri ~ _____

tu ~ _____

ha ~ _____

mu ~ _____

dri ~ _____

2. Match the word to its meaning:

grapple topple supple muzzle nuzzle tussle

able to move easily, flexible
_____

a small fight or brawl
_____

the snout or jaw of an animal
_____

to tip or tumble over
_____

to rub gently with the face or nose
_____

to try to grab hold of something
_____

3. Find the List 40 word with the closest meaning:

bother _____
wave _____
spout _____
mystery _____
glare _____

4. Write these words in alphabetical order:

nuzzle puzzle topple sizzle grizzle cripple

_____
_____
_____
_____
_____
_____

YEAR 3   WEEKS 31-40
50 Word Revision List

dazzle	cruel	grief
source	cause	scribble
mouth	blouse	apple
supple	bubble	baffle
poem	brief	kennel
shield	mould	haunt
couch	tunnel	wound
bottle	cloud	diet
sizzle	fluid	young
launch	vessel	house
pounce	group	middle
giggle	rabbit	view
parrot	puzzle	raffle
thief	shout	trouble
mound	hassle	friend
puddle	scour	kettle
priest		sauce

Complete Graded Spelling Lists with Spelling and Vocabulary Exercises

YEAR 3 LIST 41

rally
tally
jelly
silly
holly
jolly
bully
marry
berry
ferry
merry
cherry
sorry
buggy
curry
hurry

EXTRA WORDS

shaggy
lorry
gully
married
curried

1. Look at these words:

hurry + ~s = hurries
hurry + ~ed = hurried

Now try these:

marry + ~s = _____

marry + ~ed = _____

rally + ~s = _____

rally + ~ed = _____

ferry + ~s = _____

ferry + ~ed = _____

2. Which List 41 word rhymes with the proper noun in these sentences?

Ellie is eating _____.

Murray is eating _____.

Ollie is feeling _____.

Lily is feeling _____.

Laurie is saying _____.

Ali is driving in a _____.

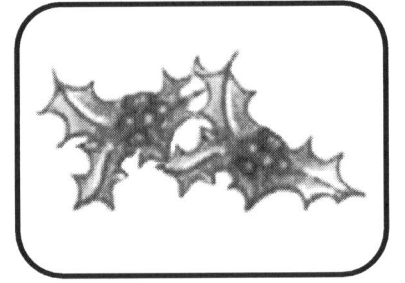

3. Choose the correct word:

fairy / ferry
fairy - a magical being
ferry - a type of boat
A _____ left a coin by my bed.
We took the _____ from the pier.

berry / bury
berry - a fruit
bury - to put under
The _____ left my fingers black.
Pirates often _____ their treasure.

4. Find the List 41 word related to:

sillier _____
jolliest _____
sorrowful _____
unmarried _____
merrier _____
unhurried _____

Complete Graded Spelling Lists with Spelling and Vocabulary Exercises

YEAR 3 LIST 42

hobby
lobby
eddy
teddy
giddy
buddy
dummy
mummy
penny
bunny
funny
happy
choppy
tatty
pretty
ditty

1. Add ~ddy or ~tty to make a List 42 word:

di ~ _____
ta ~ _____
bu ~ _____
gi ~ _____
pre ~ _____

2. Find the List 42 word with the closest meaning:

cheerful _____
friend _____
amusing _____
shabby _____
song _____
pastime _____
dizzy _____

3. Look at these words:

giddy + ~er = giddier
giddy + ~est = giddiest

Now try these:

pretty + ~er = _____

pretty + ~est = _____

funny + ~er = _____

funny + ~est = _____

choppy + ~er = _____

choppy + ~est = _____

4. Find the List 42 words with two meanings:

The _____ was prepared for burial.
- and -
Ask your _____ if you can come.

* * *

I saw the coat on the _____ in the shop.
- and -
The baby sucked hard on its _____.

EXTRA WORDS

cranny
yummy
sloppy
happily
prettily

Complete Graded Spelling Lists with Spelling and Vocabulary Exercises

YEAR 3 LIST 43

baby
ruby
lady
body
lily
holy
pity
duty
study
truly
army
party
dainty
plenty
fancy
mercy

EXTRA WORDS

balmy
dingy
lofty
grisly
surly

1. Find the List 43 word rhyming with:

newly _____
silly _____
witty _____
shady _____
buddy _____
maybe _____

2. Find the List 43 words with two meanings:

She was wearing very _____ clothes.
- and -
I don't _____ peas.

* * *

My _____ ached.
- and -
The _____ was set up to care for animals.

3. Choose the correct word:

holy / wholly
holy - sacred, divine
wholly - completely

The church is a very _____ site.
The idea was _____ his own.

4. Add ~ty or ~dy to make a List 43 word:

stu ~ _____
la ~ _____
bo ~ _____
du ~ _____
pi ~ _____

5. Look at these:

beauty + ~*full* = beaut*iful*
plenty + ~*full* = plent*iful*

Now try these:

mercy + ~*full* =
_____

plenty + ~*full* =
_____

pity + ~*full* =
_____

fancy + ~*full* =
_____

duty + ~*full* =
_____

Complete Graded Spelling Lists with Spelling and Vocabulary Exercises

YEAR 3 LIST 44

tiny
pony
puny
vary
wary
bury
fury
jury
cosy
posy
rosy
busy
ivy
navy
glory
story

3. Find the List 44 word with the closest meaning:

honour _____
weak _____
snug _____
anger _____
cautious _____
minute _____
blushing _____

1. Find the List 44 word rhyming with:

ferry _____
gravy _____
dizzy _____
loony _____
macaroni _____

4. Look at these:

envy + ~*ous* = env*i*ous
lazy + ~*ness* = laz*i*ness

Now try these:

vary + ~*ous* =
_____

glory + ~*ous* =
_____

fury + ~*ous* =
_____

busy + ~*ness* =
_____

wary + ~*ness* =
_____

cosy + ~*ness* =
_____

2. Choose the correct word:

berry / bury
berry - a fruit
bury - put underground
The _____ can be used as a dye.
The dog will _____ the bone in the garden.

story / storey
story - a tale, fiction
storey - level, floor
My room is on the fifth _____ of the house.
The _____ is too silly to be believed

EXTRA WORDS

gory
nosy
flimsy
clumsy
curtsy

49

Complete Graded Spelling Lists with Spelling and Vocabulary Exercises

YEAR 3 LIST 45

enter
banter
canter
splinter
master
plaster
fester
pester
mister
sister
blister
foster
roster
monster
cluster
fluster

EXTRA WORDS

caster
duster
muster
bluster
lobster

1. Find the List 45 word related to:

monstrous _____
pest _____
entrance _____
mistress _____
splint _____
replaster _____

2. Match the word to its meaning:

banter roster foster pester fester cluster blister

to become rotten or infected
_____

to bother or annoy
_____

to care for or support the growth of
_____

to meet or assemble
_____

a list of names, used for some purpose
_____

a bubble under the skin, filled with fluid
_____

joking or witty conversation
_____

3. Match the List 45 word to its opposite:

_____ or slave
_____ or brother
_____ or exit
_____ or gallop

4. Find the List 45 word that fits best:

to _____ a child

to _____ in groups

to put your name on a _____

to pull a _____ from your toe

to get a _____ cast on your arm

Complete Graded Spelling Lists with Spelling and Vocabulary Exercises

3. Find the List 46 word with the same letters as:

CRATE _____
BREAK _____
REPORT _____
REPLAY _____

YEAR 3
LIST 46

baker
shaker
poker
choker
cater
later
crater
grater
garter
porter
oyster
neuter
layer
player
prayer
foyer

1. Find the List 46 noun that fits best:

a salt _____
a cheese _____
a tennis _____
an _____ in a shell
a _____ around your neck
a _____ around your leg

4. Find the List 46 word that rhymes with:

tutor _____
quarter _____
square _____
lawyer _____
cloister _____

2. Find the List 46 word related to:

shakily _____
laid _____
neutrality _____
lately _____
caterer _____

5. Choose the correct word:

grater / greater
grater - something used to grate food
greater - more great

Have you seen the cheese _____?
He needs _____ confidence in himself.

EXTRA WORDS

bunker
busker
rooster
pewter
lawyer

51

YEAR 3 LIST 47

order
border
girder
murder
spider
slander
slender
tinder
ponder
blunder
plunder
thunder
boarder
former
corner
partner

EXTRA WORDS

larder
blender
farmer
formerly
orderly

1. Look at these:

cancer → cancerous
fever → feverous

Now add ~*ous* to:

slander → _____
ponder → _____
thunder → _____
murder → _____

2. Choose the correct word:

border / boarder
border - frontier
boarder - lodger

I rent my spare room out to a _____.
We needed visas to cross the _____.

3. Write these words in alphabetical order:

slender murder
plunder thunder
partner spider

_____
_____
_____
_____
_____
_____

4. Find the List 47 word that contains this word within it:

art _____
oar _____
end _____

5. Match the word to its meaning:

tinder slander ponder
former blunder
girder plunder

to think deeply _____
to raid, steal by force _____
a beam in a building _____
a silly mistake _____
twigs used for a fire _____
to insult, defame _____
prior, previous _____

Complete Graded Spelling Lists with Spelling and Vocabulary Exercises

YEAR 3 LIST 48

badger
danger
ginger
finger
linger
tiger
hunger
fever
sever
clever
river
liver
shiver
silver
hover
clover

3. Find the List 48 word with the closest meaning:

sever linger
clever fever
shiver hover

remain _____

separate _____

float _____

illness _____

tremble _____

smart _____

1. Add ~*ger* or ~*ver* to make a List 48 word:

hun ~ _____

cle ~ _____

ti ~ _____

ho ~ _____

4. Write these words in alphabetical order:

hover sever
linger liver
ginger silver

_____
_____
_____
_____
_____
_____

2. Add the List 48 noun that fits best:

_____ or toe

stupid or _____

safety or _____

_____ or tigress

_____ and gold

_____ and thirst

EXTRA WORDS

wager
burger
lever
rover
sliver

Complete Graded Spelling Lists with Spelling and Vocabulary Exercises

YEAR 3 LIST 49

paper
viper
wiper
barber
clamber
chamber
member
timber
number
slumber
hamper
tamper
scamper
temper
proper
prosper

EXTRA WORDS

amber
pamper
bumper
slumbered
prospered

1. Find the List 49 word related to:

prosperity _____

propriety _____

temperate _____

innumerable _____

viperous _____

2. Match the word to its meaning:

hamper scamper viper prosper slumber tamper timber

wood used in carpentry
_____

to be successful
_____

a large covered basket
_____

to meddle with
_____

to run playfully
_____

a poisonous snake
_____

to sleep lightly, doze
_____

3. Add ~*ber* or ~*per* to make a List 49 word:

clam ~ _____
slum ~ _____
scam ~ _____
pros ~ _____

4. Add the List 49 noun that fits best:

a phone _____
a club _____
pen and _____
a windscreen _____

5. Find the List 49 words with two meanings:

The rain will _____ the rescue attempt.
- *and* -
I've packed a picnic _____.

Complete Graded Spelling Lists with Spelling and Vocabulary Exercises

YEAR 3 LIST 50

himself
herself
anyone
anyway
anywhere
no-one
nowhere
someone
somewhere
forever
whoever
whenever
wherever
otherwise
meanwhile
therefore

EXTRA WORDS

yourselves
themselves
nobody
anybody
somebody

---

1. Word maths:

no + one =

_____

where + ever =

_____

---

2. Add the word that fits best:

where whereas anywhere nowhere whereby somewhere wherever everywhere whereabouts

I like green, _____ you like red.
The man's _____ were still unknown.
The hall is full; there is _____ to sit.
I've looked _____ for my glasses.

3. Place these List 50 words:

whether forever nowhere whoever somewhere someone

_____ and ever
_____ or not
_____ or other
_____ to be seen
_____ you may be
_____ over the rainbow

---

4. Find the List 50 word rhyming with:

door   _____
buys   _____
style   _____
prey   _____

---

5. Put these words together to make six List 50 words:

other way ever any one fore there while who wise mean no-

_____ _____
_____ _____
_____ _____

YEAR 3   WEEKS 41-50
50 Word Revision List

story	murder	prayer
proper	anyone	fury
whenever	truly	marry
cherry	sister	splinter
temper	hobby	no-one
otherwise	busy	tiny
porter	pretty	happy
layer	later	clever
boarder	cluster	baby
scamper	sorry	forever
master	rosy	jolly
bury	thunder	neuter
somewhere	body	dainty
tiger	danger	shiver
funny	wherever	meanwhile
paper	mercy	chamber
ditty		lady

Complete Graded Spelling Lists with Spelling and Vocabulary Exercises

YEAR FOUR

List 1	Words for numbers
Lists 2-5	Words ending in ~*le*
List 6	Words with *ck*
List 7	Words ending in ~*et*
Lists 8-13	Words ending in a single consonant
List 14	Words ending in ~*ic*
List 15	Words ending in ~*id*
Lists 16-17	Words ending in ~*al*
List 18	Words ending in ~*el* or ~*il*
List 19	Words ending in ~*el* or ~*ol*
List 20	Words ending in ~*ial*
List 21	Words ending in ~*y*
List 22	Words ending in ~*ay* or ~*oy*
List 23	Words with *x* and *z*
Lists 24-25	Words with *qu*
List 26	Words starting with *wh*~
List 27	Words with *ph*
Lists 28-29	Words with silent letters
List 30	Words with *igh*
List 31	Words with *ough*
List 32	Words starting with *wr*~
Lists 33-35	Words with unusual vowel sounds
List 36	Words with *ow*
List 37	Words ending in ~*ow*, ~*ew* and ~*aw*
List 38	Words with *ai*
List 39	Words with *ea*
List 40	Words with *ie*
List 41	Words with *ei*
List 42	Words with *ui*
List 43	Words with common prefixes: *a*~ and *ad*~
List 44	Words with common prefixes: *com*~ and *con*~
List 45	Words with common prefixes: *de*~ and *dis*~
List 46	Words with common prefixes: *ex*~, *im*~ and *in*~
List 47	Words with common prefixes: *per*~, *pre*~ and *pro*~
List 48	Words with common prefixes: *re*~
List 49	Words for days and numbers
List 50	Words for times of the day or year

Complete Graded Spelling Lists with Spelling and Vocabulary Exercises

YEAR 4 LIST 1

eleven
twelve
thirteen
fourteen
fifteen
sixteen
seventeen
eighteen
nineteen
twenty
thirty
forty
fifty
hundred
thousand
million
billion
twenty-one

EXTRA WORDS

trillion
thirty-two
forty-three
millionth
billionth

---

1. Find the List 1 word that rhymes with:

naughty — *twenty*
dirty — *forty*
plenty — *thirty*
delve — *twelve*
heaven — *eleven*
thrifty — *fifty*

2. Add ~*ty* or ~*teen* to make a List 1 word:

for ~ — *ty*
twen ~ — *ty*
four ~ — *teen*

3. Find the List 1 word that contains this word within it:

net — *nineteen*
and — *thousand*
vent — *seventn*
eve — *seventeen*
went — *twenty*
if — *fifty*

4. Complete these sums with List 1 words:

five times three equals *fifteen*

half of forty-two equals *twenty-one*

thirty-six divided by two equals *eighteen*

seventy-five minus forty-five equals ____

eighty divided by two equals *four*

sixteen minus two equals *fourteen*

ten times one hundred equals one *ten*

Complete Graded Spelling Lists with Spelling and Vocabulary Exercises

YEAR 4 LIST 2

able
cable
fable
table
stable
bible
noble
marble
feeble
gamble
scramble
tremble
nimble
thimble
humble
mumble
crumble
stumble

EXTRA WORDS

ramble
treble
fumble
rumble
grumble

1. Add ~ble or ~mble to make a List 2 word:

sta ~ _ble_
ni ~ _mble_
hu ~ _mble_
stu ~ _mble_
bi ~ _ble_

2. Find the List 2 words with two meanings:

She saw her hopes _crumble_ when she lost the semi-final.
- and -
We ate apple _crumble_ with cream.

* * *

We had to _stumble_ over the rocky ground as best we could.
- and -
The spies _stumble_ their messages before sending them.

3. Add the List 2 verb that fits best:

to _tremble_ in the cold
to _stumble_ over your feet
to _muble_ your lines in a play
to _gamble_ away your savings

4. Find the List 2 word with the closest meaning:

upright _able_
tale _fable_
shiver _tremble_
agile _nimble_
modest _noble_
steady _stable_

5. Place the correct word in the sentence:

able ability disabled disability unable inability

I'm sorry I'm _unable_ to go to the party.
No-one doubted her musical _ability_.
I have a _disability_: my hearing is very poor.

Complete Graded Spelling Lists with Spelling and Vocabulary Exercises

YEAR 4 LIST 3

ladle
cradle
needle
candle
handle
kindle
fondle
bundle
ample
sample
temple
dimple
simple
staple
steeple
people
triple
purple

EXTRA WORDS

maple
spindle
dwindle
cradling
sampling

1. Which List 3 word does this mnemonic teach?

P_P_e_o_ple
Prefer _e_ ating
_O_utdoors

2. Look at these:

cradle → cradling
handle → handling

Now add ~ing to:

triple → _tripling_
kindle → _kindling_
sample → _sampling_

3. Find the List 3 words with two meanings:

Please _staple_ the papers together.
- and -
Bread is the _staple_ food in their diet.

* * *

Pull the _handle_ hard to close the door.
- and -
Can you _handle_ so many children in your house?

4. Add the List 3 word that fits best:

simple or difficult
double or _triple_
needle and thread
candle wax
a church _steeple_
a baby's _cradle_
a crowd of _people_

5. Find the List 3 word with the closest meaning:

shrine — _temple_
model — _sample_
caress — _fondle_
package — _bundle_
easy — _simple_
threefold — _triple_
plenty — _ample_

Complete Graded Spelling Lists with Spelling and Vocabulary Exercises

3. Add ~*gle* or ~*tle* to make a List 4 word:

sin ~ _gle_
bus ~ _tle_
tur ~ _tle_
bur ~ _gle_
star ~ _tle_

YEAR 4 LIST 4

- angle
- bangle
- dangle
- tangle
- strangle
- jingle
- mingle
- single
- burgle
- gurgle
- title
- beetle
- startle
- turtle
- castle
- nestle
- bustle
- rustle

1. Add the List 4 noun that fits best:

gurgle of a baby
bustle of a crowd
rustle of leaves

4. Find the List 4 word with two meanings:

The team won the _title_ for the third year running.
- and -
Do you know the book's _title_?

2. What am I? Find the List 4 noun:

I live in a shell: _turtle_
I have six legs: _beetle_
I'm worn on a wrist: _bangle_
I'm found in hair: _tangle_
I'm found on a hill: _castle_
I'm found on a book: _title_

5. Find the List 4 word related to:

entangled _tangle_
entitled _title_
angular _angle_
singular _single_
burglary _burgle_
strangulation _strangle_

EXTRA WORDS

- mangle
- tingle
- mantle
- jostle
- hurtle

61

YEAR 4 LIST 5

trifle
stifle
ankle
sparkle
twinkle
sprinkle
cackle
tackle
crackle
shackle
freckle
fickle
pickle
tickle
prickle
trickle
buckle
chuckle

EXTRA WORDS

rifle
crinkle
heckle
suckle
speckled

1. Add the List 5 word that fits best:

a _trickle_ of water

a _sprinkle_ of salt

the ~~twinkle~~ _sparkle_ of a star

the _sparkle_ of clean teeth

a _chuckle_ of laughter

a _freckle_ on your face

the _crackle_ of a fire

2. Find the List 5 words with two meanings:

I've made a huge _trifle_ to feed all the children.
- and -
It was a _trifle_ to pay for such a lovely day out.

* * *

The old tennis racquets would _buckle_ when they got wet.
- and -
Her dress has a fancy _buckle_ at the waist.

3. Add ~ickle or ~inkle to make a List 5 word:

f ~ _ickle_

pr ~ _ickle_

tw ~ _inkle_

spr ~ _inkle_

tr ~ _ickle_

4. Find the List 5 word related to:

pricked _prickle_

cracking _crackle_

unbuckled _buckle_

sparky _sparkle_

anklet _ankle_

unshackling _shackle_

Complete Graded Spelling Lists with Spelling and Vocabulary Exercises

YEAR 4 LIST 6

beckon
reckon
bicker
wicker
sticker
jacket
packet
racket
bracket
ticket
wicket
thicket
cricket
locket
pocket
rocket
socket
bucket

3. Add ~cker or ~cket to make a List 6 word:

cri ~ _cket_
sti ~ _cker_
bu ~ _cket_
bi ~ _cker_
thi ~ _cket_

1. What am I? Find the List 6 noun:

I fly to the moon: _rocket_
I'm worn around your neck: _locket_
I'm worn over your clothes: _jacket_
I'm used to carry water: _bucket_
I'm found in your trousers: _pocket_

4. Look at these:

beckon → beckoned
pocket → pocketed
nicker → nickered

Now add ~ed to:

bracket → _bracketed_
ticket → _ticketed_
bicker → _bickered_
rocket → _rocketed_
reckon → _reckoned_

2. Add the List 6 word that fits best:

a _packet_ of crisps
a _ticket_ to a show
a _wicker_ chair
a plug in a _socket_
a _sticker_ on your windscreen

5. Choose the correct word:

racket / racquet
racket - loud noises
racquet - for playing sports

Bring your _racquet_ and we will play tennis. Who is making the _racket_ in the hall?

EXTRA WORDS

cracker
docket
picket
bracketed
pocketed

63

Complete Graded Spelling Lists with Spelling and Vocabulary Exercises

YEAR 4 LIST 7

- cadet
- target
- forget
- basket
- blanket
- tablet
- triplet
- violet
- toilet
- racquet
- helmet
- magnet
- planet
- carpet
- trumpet
- secret
- closet
- velvet

EXTRA WORDS

- casket
- trinket
- hatchet
- goblet
- bracelet

1. Add the List 7 noun that fits best:

a tennis _racquet_
a shopping _basket_
an army _cadet_
a blocked _toilet_
a bicycle _helmet_

2. Look at these:

pocket → pocketing
closet → closeting

Now add ~*ing* to:

carpet → _carpeting_

trumpet → _trumpeting_

blanket → _blanketing_

target → _targeting_

3. Find the List 7 word with two meanings:

The soft _blanket_ was warm and cosy.
- *and* -
There is a _blanket_ ban on ball games.

4. Complete the List 7 words:

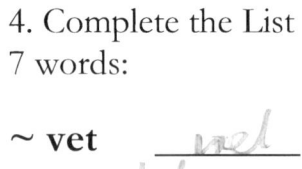

~ vet _vel_
~ met _hel mo_
~ set _clo_
~ det _ca_
~ ret _sec_

5. Word maths:

magnet + ~*ic* = _magnetic_

secret + ~*ive* = _secretive_

velvet + ~*een* = _velveteen_

trumpet + ~*er* = _trumpeter_

toilet + ~*ry* + ~*s* = _toiletrys_

forget + ~*full* = _forgetfull_

toiletries

Complete Graded Spelling Lists with Spelling and Vocabulary Exercises

3. Add ~*an* or ~*it* to make a List 8 word:

ed ~ _it_
turb ~ _an_
perm ~ _it_
hum ~ _an_
spir ~ _it_

YEAR 4
LIST 8

urban
turban
organ
human
habit
orbit
edit
credit
digit
limit
hermit
permit
unit
merit
spirit
culprit
robot
pivot

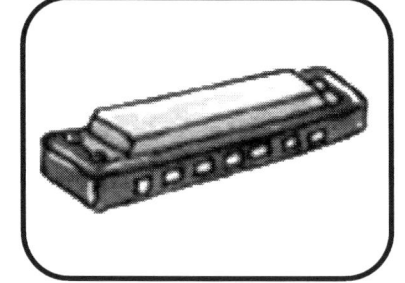

1. Add the List 8 noun that fits best:

a mouth _____
a _human_ being
a planet's _orbit_
a parking _permit_
a _credit_ card
a speed _limit_

4. Find the List 8 word that rhymes most closely with:

rabbit _habit_
rivet _pivot_
inherit _merit_

2. Find the List 8 words with two meanings:

This phone number is missing its last _digit_.
- and -
I could not move a single _digit_ on my hand.

* * *

Let's go to an _organ_ recital at the town hall.
- and -
The lung is a vital _organ_ of the body.

5. Look at these:

edit + ~*ed* = edited
edit + ~*ing* = editing

Now try these:

limit + ~*ed* =
limited
limit + ~*ing* =
limiting
orbit + ~*ed* =
orbited
orbit + ~*ing* =
orbiting

EXTRA WORDS

bigot
pagan
emit
spirited
merited

65

Complete Graded Spelling Lists with Spelling and Vocabulary Exercises

YEAR 4 LIST 9

burden
garden
linen
open
siren
children
haven
raven
heaven
kitchen
cabin
robin
napkin
pumpkin
violin
basin
raisin
satin

1. Add ~*en* or ~*in* to make a List 9 word:

rav ~ _en_
rais ~ _in_
heav ~ _en_
sir ~ _en_
napk ~ _in_

2. Find the List 9 word closest in meaning to:

paradise _heaven_
weight _burden_
refuge _haven_
serviette _napkin_
alarm _siren_
unfasten _open_

3. Write these words in alphabetical order:

kitchen heaven raven pumpkin raisin napkin

heaven
napkin
pumpkin
raisin
raven
kitchen

EXTRA WORDS

token
goblin
omen
vermin
vitamin

4. What am I? Find the List 9 noun:

I am full of plants and flowers: _garden_
I am a place where food is cooked: _garden_ _napkin_
I am a large orange vegetable: _pumkin_
I am a musical instrument: _violin_
I am a large black bird: _raven_

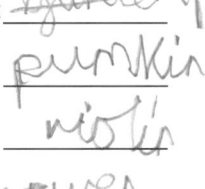

Complete Graded Spelling Lists with Spelling and Vocabulary Exercises

YEAR 4 LIST 10

icon
bacon
pardon
wagon
dragon
salon
melon
nylon
demon
lemon
cannon
iron
apron
crimson
person
baton
crayon
canyon

EXTRA WORDS

flagon
colon
coupon
heron
prison

1. Find the List 10 word that contains this word within it:

rag — dragon
any — canyon
don — pardon
rim — crimson
ray — crayon

2. Add the List 10 word that fits best:

to fire a — bacon
to drive a — wagon
to ___ a shirt — iron
to wear an — apron
to draw with a — crayon
to beg someone's — apron

3. Match the words to their meaning:

salon demon baton icon canyon nylon

a synthetic material — icon
a place where a hairdresser works — salon
a evil spirit or devil — demon
a deep gorge or ravine — canyon
a stick or short rod — baton
a religious object — nylon

4. Word maths:

icon + ~ic = iconic
demon + ~ize = demonize
wagon + ~er = wagoner
iron + ~ing = ironing
person + ~al + ~ity = personality

YEAR 4   WEEKS 1-10
50 Word Revision List

children	buckle	castle
packet	dragon	forty
crimson	violet	fourteen
orbit	spirit	needle
fable	thousand	cannon
jacket	crayon	robot
nylon	pocket	kitchen
human	billion	tremble
violin	stifle	sample
secret	crumble	turtle
crackle	single	ankle
heaven	bacon	racquet
gurgle	sprinkle	eighteen
reckon	habit	haven
digit	purple	beetle
basket	noble	pumpkin
people		rocket

YEAR 4 LIST 11

item
denim
victim
atom
venom
seldom
random
wisdom
freedom
ransom
custom
forum
album
emblem
problem
pilgrim
spectrum
tantrum

EXTRA WORDS

totem
maxim
fathom
tandem
mayhem

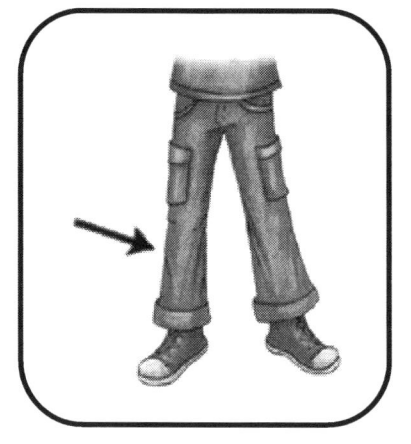

1. Find the List 11 word that contains this word within it:

and _____
reed _____
ant _____
rim _____
rob _____

2. Find the List 11 word closest in meaning to:

payoff _____
infrequent _____
tradition _____
logo _____
outburst _____
difficulty _____
haphazard _____

3. Place the correct word in the sentence:

wise wiser wisest wisely unwisely wisdom

He is the _____ person I know.
He always speaks and acts _____.
He is known for the _____ of his actions.
He says that it is _____ to stay silent than to speak rashly.

4. Complete the table with a List 11 word:

Adjective	Noun
wise	_____
free	_____
venomous	_____
problematic	_____
emblematic	_____
customary	_____

YEAR 4 LIST 12

superb
proverb
shepherd
modern
lantern
pattern
cavern
govern
tavern
inert
overt
concert
expert
assert
insert
covert
convert
subvert

EXTRA WORDS

berserk
discern
cistern
lectern
revert

1. Some prefixes have meanings:

con = with, around
in = in, into
ex = from, out of
sub = under
super = above

Now add a List 12 word that means:

to undermine _____

to place inside _____

above the ordinary _____

knowledge gained out of experience _____

music, played with others _____

to change, turn around _____

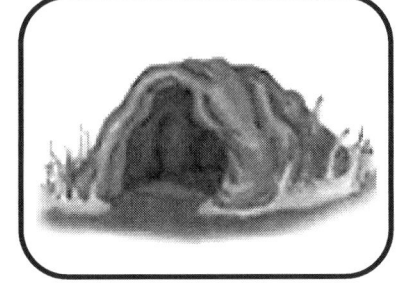

2. Find the List 12 word related to:

Verb	Noun
_____	assertion
_____	insertion
_____	subversion
_____	conversion
_____	government

3. Add ~*ern* or ~*ert* to make a List 12 word:

ov ~ _____
patt ~ _____
cov ~ _____
in ~ _____
cav ~ _____

4. Match the word to its meaning:

assert convert covert subvert proverb overt

a common saying _____

open for all to see _____

to change someone's opinion _____

closed, secretive _____

to undermine, disrupt _____

to proclaim, declare _____

Complete Graded Spelling Lists with Spelling and Vocabulary Exercises

3. Find the List 13 word that contains this word within it:

hop _____

lip _____

urn _____

rook _____

acre _____

YEAR 4 LIST 13

ragged
dogged
rugged
wicked
crooked
sacred
hatred
kindred
method
period
serif
motif
tulip
turnip
parsnip
gossip
gallop
bishop

1. Add the List 13 word that fits best:

a _____ hymn

a _____ of time

a _____ in a cathedral

2. Match the word to its meaning:

ragged dogged serif motif rugged kindred

tough, strong, craggy
_____

a theme in a piece of writing or music
_____

stubborn, persistent
_____

worn out from use
_____

of the same family
_____

small lines in a typeface _____

4. Match the List 13 word to its opposite:

love or _____

straight or _____

good or _____

neat or _____

trot or _____

5. Find the List 13 word that is related to:

periodical
_____

methodical
_____

sacrificial
_____

EXTRA WORDS

naked
scallop
dollop
methodical
periodical

71

YEAR 4 LIST 14

mimic
comic
panic
sonic
tonic
topic
music
basic
critic
attic
toxic
ethic
traffic
italic
frolic
garlic
public
hectic

EXTRA WORDS

cubic
relic
antic
mimicking
panicking

1. Find the List 14 word related to:

publicity _____
toxicity _____
basically _____
unethically _____

2. Complete the table:

Noun	Adjective
_____	critical
_____	topical
ethic	_____
comic	_____

3. Place the correct word in the sentence:

critic critical criticism critically criticize uncritical uncritically

He is always so _____ of me.
He is always trying to _____ me.
He always speaks _____ of me.
His _____ of me never ends.

4. Find the List 14 word closest in meaning to:

funny _____
plain _____
alarm _____
romp _____
loft _____
frantic _____

5. Add List 14 words to the table:

Noun	Adjective
base	_____
toxin	_____
comedy	_____
sound	_____

Complete Graded Spelling Lists with Spelling and Vocabulary Exercises

YEAR 4 LIST 15

acid
placid
lucid
rigid
frigid
valid
solid
timid
humid
rapid
stupid
horrid
putrid
livid
vivid
morbid
sordid
splendid

3. Add ~*cid* or ~*lid* to make a List 15 word:

lu ~ _____
va ~ _____
so ~ _____
pla ~ _____

1. Place the correct word in the sentence:

**valid validity
validation validly
validate validation
invalid invalidity**

He presented a perfectly _____ argument.
He gave an argument to _____ his claim.
The _____ of his argument was evident.

4. Match the List 15 word to its opposite:

clever or _____
slow or _____
dry or _____
dull or _____

5. Match the word to its meaning:

**putrid livid lucid
rigid morbid placid**

very angry _____
unmoving _____
rotting, decayed _____
clear and bright _____
gloomy, sullen _____
calm, docile, timid _____

2. Complete the table:

Adjective	Noun
_____	rigidity
_____	timidity
lucid	_____
stupid	_____
acid	_____

EXTRA WORDS

rabid
acrid
torrid
rigidity
stupidity

YEAR 4 LIST 16

focal
local
vocal
medal
pedal
legal
regal
frugal
canal
final
oral
coral
moral
floral
spiral
mural
rural
plural

EXTRA WORDS

verbal
bridal
feudal
feral
rascal

1. Add ~*cal* or ~*ral* to make a List 16 word:

mu ~ _____
mo ~ _____
vo ~ _____
flo ~ _____
lo ~ _____

2. Add the List 16 word that fits best:

_____ on a wall
_____ of a story
_____ in the sea
_____ on a bike
_____ of honour

3. Add List 16 words to the table:

Noun	Adjective
finish	_____
spire	_____
voice	_____
focus	_____
locality	_____
flower	_____

4. Look at these:

plural → plurality
frugal → frugality

Now add ~ity to:

moral → _____
legal → _____
local → _____

5. Place the correct word in the sentence:

**voice voiced voicing
voiceless vocalized
vocal vocalist vocally**

She likes to _____ her opinions.
She is the _____ for a jazz band.
She does exercises to strengthen her _____ chords.

Complete Graded Spelling Lists with Spelling and Vocabulary Exercises

YEAR 4 LIST 17

sandal
scandal
formal
normal
petal
metal
vital
total
mental
mortal
oval
rival
loyal
royal
animal
several
hospital
festival

3. Add ~*mal* or ~*tal* to make a List 17 word:

men ~ _____
for ~ _____
to ~ _____
mor ~ _____
nor ~ _____

1. Find the List 17 word that means:

regular _____
opponent _____
entire _____
outrage _____
faithful _____
imperial _____

4. Match the word to a prefix to make its opposite:

dis~ im~ in~

mortal _____
loyal _____
formal _____

2. Find the List 17 word that is related to:

abnormally
_____
revitalize
_____
inhospitable
_____

5. Add ~*ty* or ~*ity* to make a new word:

formal + ? = _____
royal + ? = _____
vital + ? = _____
loyal + ? = _____
mortal + ? = _____

EXTRA WORDS

dismal
fatal
brutal
totality
mortality

YEAR 4 LIST 18

label
rebel
lapel
chapel
repel
easel
weasel
tinsel
tassel
hotel
pastel
pencil
pupil
peril
fossil
devil
nostril
fulfil

EXTRA WORDS

morsel
vigil
basil
tonsil
tendril

1. Find the List 18 word related to:

fossilized _____
perilous _____
repulsive _____
rebellious _____

2. Find the List 18 word with two meanings:

The _____ of his eye is damaged.
- and -
She is a _____ of the maths tutor.

3. Look at these:

repel + ~ed = repelled
repel + ~ing = repelling

Now try these:

rebel + ~ed = _____

rebel + ~ing = _____

fulfil + ~ed = _____

fulfil + ~ing = _____

4. Add ~el or ~il to make a List 18 word:

past ~ _____
tass ~ _____
tins ~ _____
nostr ~ _____
lap ~ _____

5. What am I? Find the List 18 noun:

I am very old: _____
I am very evil: _____
I am used for painting: _____
I am used for praying: _____
I am used on holidays: _____
I am used for breathing: _____
I am used for writing: _____

YEAR 4 LIST 19

cancel
parcel
model
camel
kernel
level
revel
swivel
hovel
novel
travel
marvel
jewel
idol
carol
patrol
petrol
control

EXTRA WORDS

libel
gospel
navel
gravel
grovel

1. Find the List 19 word rhyming with:

fuel _____
unravel _____
barrel _____
eternal _____
waddle _____
sidle _____

2. Choose the correct word:

colonel / kernel
colonel - army leader
kernel - the nut or core

There is a _____ of truth in her words.
The _____ gave the order to hold rank.

idle / idol
idle - lazy
idol - object of worship

I was _____ for an hour while I waited.
The tribe's _____ is a giant snake.

3. Match the word to its meaning:

patrol novel marvel swivel revel hovel

a story in book form
_____

to be amazed at
_____

to turn on the spot
_____

to party, to celebrate
_____

a poor, dirty house
_____

to keep watch over
_____

4. Look at these:

revel + ~ed = reve**ll**ed
revel + ~ing = reve**ll**ing

Now try these:

swivel + ~*ed* = _____

control + ~*ing* = _____

patrol + ~*ed* = _____

level + ~*ing* = _____

marvel + ~*ed* = _____

travel + ~*ing* = _____

Complete Graded Spelling Lists with Spelling and Vocabulary Exercises

YEAR 4 LIST 20

dial
trial
special
social
crucial
official
cordial
genial
menial
serial
burial
partial
spatial
jovial
trivial
material
initial
essential

EXTRA WORDS

memorial
tutorial
potential
triviality
joviality

1. Add ~*cial* or ~*tial* to make a List 20 word:

spe ~ _____
ini ~ _____
cru ~ _____
offi ~ _____
spa ~ _____

2. Add List 20 words to the table:

Noun	Adjective
part	_____
office	_____
matter	_____
trivia	_____
society	_____
essence	_____

3. Choose the correct word:

cereal / serial
cereal - a grain
serial - a broadcast series

I watch a television _____ every day.
Which _____ do you eat for breakfast?

4. Match the word to a prefix to make its opposite:

un~ im~ in~

material _____
official _____
essential _____

5. Match the word to its meaning:

trivial menial crucial
genial jovial spatial

to do with space
_____
cheery, happy
_____
work that is humble
_____
friendly, warm
_____
unimportant
_____
vital
_____

YEAR 4   WEEKS 11-20
50 Word Revision List

splendid	rugged	problem
jewel	horrid	royal
initial	convert	victim
carol	toxic	swivel
moral	burial	vivid
repel	seldom	gallop
crucial	parcel	official
music	public	spectrum
festival	hatred	ethic
spiral	normal	panic
lantern	concert	wicked
frugal	shepherd	superb
period	essential	plural
pencil	hospital	several
frigid	motif	pupil
wisdom	material	custom
focal		placid

YEAR 4 LIST 21

ugly
envy
treaty
empty
beauty
family
enemy
colony
misery
sanity
vanity
purity
cavity
gravity
liberty
property
poverty
galaxy

EXTRA WORDS

legacy
fallacy
canopy
canary
embassy

1. Add ~*ity* or ~*erty* to make a List 21 word:

prop ~ _____
lib ~ _____
cav ~ _____
van ~ _____
pov ~ _____

2. Add List 21 words to the table:

Adjective	Noun
poor	_____
grave	_____
sane	_____
vain	_____
envious	_____

3. Find the List 21 word closest in meaning to:

freedom _____
unfilled _____
belongings _____
jealousy _____
rationality _____
cleanliness _____

4. Find the List 21 word with two meanings:

In space, there is no _____.
- and -
He didn't understand the _____ of the situation.

5. Choose the correct word:

family familial familiar familiarize familiarity unfamiliar unfamiliarity

His _____ is very wealthy.
He looks _____ but I don't know who he is.
My _____ with French helped me in Paris.
I tried to _____ myself with the city.

Complete Graded Spelling Lists with Spelling and Vocabulary Exercises

YEAR 4 LIST 22

allay
array
essay
hooray
delay
mislay
dismay
display
astray
betray
portray
decoy
enjoy
annoy
convoy
deploy
employ
destroy

EXTRA WORDS

foray
heyday
outlay
betrayal
portrayal

1. Add ~*ay* or ~*oy* to make a List 22 word:

   del ~ _____

   ann ~ _____

   dism ~ _____

   arr ~ _____

   destr ~ _____

2. Find the List 22 word that fits best:

   to shout _____

   to _____ music

   to _____ staff

   to write an _____

   to _____ someone's fears

   to _____ someone's trust

3. Match the word to its meaning:

   convoy deploy astray
   allay betray array

   to be disloyal
   _____

   a line of vehicles
   _____

   amiss, lost
   _____

   to put into action
   _____

   to calm or lessen
   _____

   a spread or display
   _____

4. Add ~*al* or ~*ment* to make the noun of these verbs:

   employ + ? =
   _____

   enjoy + ? =
   _____

   portray + ? =
   _____

   betray + ? =
   _____

   deploy + ? =
   _____

Complete Graded Spelling Lists with Spelling and Vocabulary Exercises

YEAR 4 LIST 23

vex
relax
index
flux
zone
zero
zebra
zigzag
hazel
dizzy
frenzy
bronze
frieze
snooze
blazer
trapeze
bazaar
bizarre

EXTRA WORDS

apex
annex
fizzy
gauze
tweezers

1. Choose the correct word:

bazaar / bizarre
bazaar - a fete, market
bizarre - very strange

A _____ sight met my eyes.
I bought a china mug at the _____.

freeze / frieze
freeze - grow cold
frieze - a decoration around a room's walls

The _____ was too high up to see.
I'll _____ the pie and eat it next week.

2. What am I? Find the List 23 noun:

I am a metal: _____

I am nothing: _____

I have four legs: _____

I am a brown colour: _____

I am used in a circus: _____

I am very crooked: _____

I keep you warm: _____

I am alphabetical: _____

3. Word maths:

relax + ~*ed* = _____

frenzy + ~*ed* = _____

snooze + ~*ing* = _____

dizzy + ~*ing* = _____

4. Match the word to its meaning:

flux   blazer   index
hazel   frenzy   vex

a file, an ordered list _____

a soft brown colour _____

to worry or irritate _____

a formal jacket _____

a state of turmoil _____

a state of change _____

Complete Graded Spelling Lists with Spelling and Vocabulary Exercises

$$\frac{1}{2} = \frac{2}{4}$$

1. Choose the correct word:

<u>cue / queue</u>
cue - a prompt
queue - a waiting line

It was her _____ to go to the stage.
There is a _____ about a mile long.

2. Word maths:

quarry + ~s = _____

quantity + ~s = _____

qualify + ~s = _____

3. Place these words:

query enquire question

I will ask a _____.
I will pose a _____.
I will _____ about something.

4. Find the List 24 word that rhymes with:

shiver _____
dribble _____
sorry _____
moral _____
through _____
work _____
sequel _____

5. Match the word to its meaning:

quarry quartet query queasy quirk quibble quiver

a pit from which minerals are mined
_____

nauseous, feeling sick
_____

a question or inquiry
_____

four musicians
_____

to tremble, shake
_____

a slight objection
_____

a strange attitude or habit
_____

YEAR 4 LIST 24

queue
quirk
quarry
quarrel
quarter
quartet
query
queasy
question
quibble
quiver
qualify
quality
quantity
equal
tranquil
enquire
require

EXTRA WORDS

quartz
queued
qualified
quarrelled
quivered

Complete Graded Spelling Lists with Spelling and Vocabulary Exercises

YEAR 4 LIST 25

squad
squat
square
squash
squeeze
squeak
squeal
squid
squint
squire
squirm
squirt
squabble
squalor
squander
squirrel
liquid
conquer

EXTRA WORDS

squall
squelch
squatting
squeezing
squirreling

1. Find the List 25 word that means:

waste _____
overcome _____
wriggle _____
team _____
short _____

2. Word maths:

squat + ~*ing* =
_____

squeeze + ~*ing* =
_____

squeal + ~*ing* =
_____

3. What am I? Find the List 25 noun:

I live in the sea:
_____

I work for a knight:
_____

I have four legs:
_____

I have four sides:
_____

I am neither a solid nor a gas:
_____

4. Find the List 25 word with two meanings:

We played three games of _____.
 - *and* -
Can we all _____ in to the back seat of the car?

5. Find the List 25 word that rhymes with:

hurt _____
wheel _____
wobble _____
term _____
hair _____
pot _____
tyre _____

Complete Graded Spelling Lists with Spelling and Vocabulary Exercises

YEAR 4 LIST 26

whack
wharf
whet
wheat
whence
whiff
whilst
whine
whirl
wheedle
whimper
whimsy
whinny
whisker
whisper
whistle
whittle
whereas

EXTRA WORDS

whoop
whopper
whirling
whining
whistling

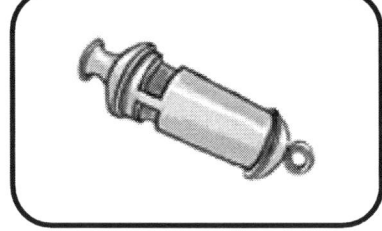

1. Choose the correct word:

wet / whet
wet - not dry
whet - to increase or sharpen

The smell of food _____ my appetite.
I slipped on the _____ leaves.

whine / wine
wine - a drink
whine - to complain

He pulled the cork from the _____.
The dog's _____ gets on my nerves.

2. Find the List 26 word that rhymes with:

sense _____
complete _____
sign _____
flimsy _____
curl _____

3. Write these words in alphabetical order:

whine whisker whittle whirl whiff whilst

_____
_____
_____
_____
_____
_____

4. Match the word to its meaning:

whimper wheedle whence whinny whack whimsy whittle

sound of a horse
_____

to use a knife to make a shape from wood
_____

good humour
_____

to cajole something from someone
_____

a thud or thwack
_____

to cry or sob quietly
_____

from where _____

85

Complete Graded Spelling Lists with Spelling and Vocabulary Exercises

YEAR 4 LIST 27

phase
phrase
phone
phantom
pharaoh
phoenix
physics
physical
sphere
sphinx
orphan
dolphin
elephant
emphasis
triumph
trophy
graph
photograph

EXTRA WORDS

phobia
pheasant
periphery
autograph
telegraph

1. Place the correct word in the sentence:

emphasis emphasize emphasizing emphatic emphatically

He kept _____ that we must take care.
He was most _____ that we must take care.
He told us to take care most _____.

2. Find the List 27 word that means:

victory _____
chart _____
bodily _____
stress _____
expression _____
ball _____
award _____

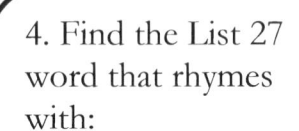

3. Choose the correct word:

<u>faze / phase</u>
faze - to overwhelm
phase - a stage, time

He is entering a difficult _____ in his life.
The noise does not seem to _____ him.

4. Find the List 27 word that rhymes with:

sinks _____
bingo _____
groan _____
icicle _____

5. What am I? Find the List 27 noun:

I have no parents:
_____

I am half human:
_____

I am a ghost or spirit:
_____

I am an unusual bird:
_____

I am an ancient king:
_____

I am taught at school:
_____

Complete Graded Spelling Lists with Spelling and Vocabulary Exercises

YEAR 4 LIST 28

soften
fasten
hasten
listen
glisten
moisten
island
knack
knee
kneel
knelt
knead
knit
knife
knob
knot
knock
knuckle

EXTRA WORDS

knell
knoll
knave
softened
fastened

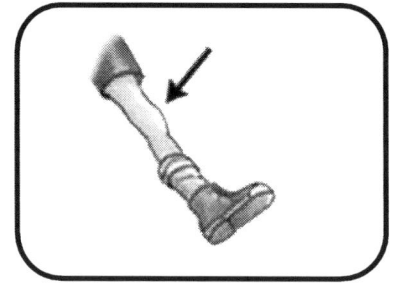

1. Find the List 28 verb that fits best:

to _____ at a door
to _____ to music
to _____ dough
to _____ a seatbelt

2. Look at these words:

soft + ~en + ~ed = softened
soft + ~en + ~ing = softening

Now try these:

moist + ~en + ~ed =
_____

moist + ~en + ~ing =
_____

haste + ~en + ~ed =
_____

haste + ~en + ~ing =
_____

fast + ~en + ~ed =
_____

fast + ~en + ~ing =
_____

3. Choose the correct word:

need / knead
I _____ more sleep.
You must _____ the dough for five minutes.

not / knot
There is a _____ in my shoelaces.
I told you _____ to go swimming.

nit / knit
My mother likes to _____ clothing.
A _____ is a tiny louse.

4. Find three List 28 words from the same word family:

_____ _____ _____

5. Place the correct word in the sentence:

fast fasten faster fastest fastener fastening unfasten

He is _____ than I.
She is the _____ in the school.
I broke the _____ on my purse.

87

YEAR 4 LIST 29

sign
lamb
limb
climb
bomb
comb
tomb
dumb
numb
crumb
thumb
debt
doubt
subtle
yacht
stalk
column
answer

EXTRA WORDS

design
resign
psalm
almond
salmon

---

1. Find the List 29 verb that fits best:

to _____ a hill

to _____ your hair

to _____ a question

to _____ your own ability

---

2. Find the List 29 noun that fits best:

a _____ of bread

a _____ at sea

a street _____

the _____ on your hand

---

3. Choose the correct word:

stork / stalk
stork - a type of bird
stalk - a stem
- or -
stalk - to follow, trail

My cat is happy to _____ birds all day.
I like to eat a _____ of celery.
The _____ was standing on one leg.

---

4. Find the List 29 word with:

a silent *g* : _____

a silent *ch* : _____

a silent *w* : _____

a silent *n* : _____

a silent *l* : _____

---

5. Find the List 29 word that rhymes with:

forget _____

apricot _____

scout _____

home _____

hymn _____

fine _____

Complete Graded Spelling Lists with Spelling and Vocabulary Exercises

YEAR 4 LIST 30

high
sigh
thigh
bight
fight
light
might
night
right
sight
tight
bright
flight
fright
plight
slight
height
knight

EXTRA WORDS

blight
lightning
brightening
frightening
tightening

---

3. Match the List 30 word to its opposite:

_____ or low
day or _____
wrong or _____
dim or _____
loose or _____
dark or _____
blindness or _____

1. Complete these with a List 30 word:

to be as _____ as a button
to be the _____ of fashion
to be scared of a bump in the _____

---

4. Find the List 30 words with two meanings:

He had the _____ of the army behind him.
- and -
I think I _____ be late home tonight.

* * *

Turn _____ on the next street.
- and -
He has no _____ to speak to you that way

* * *

Turn on the _____ if you want to read your book.
- and -
The bag is _____ and easy to carry.

---

2. Choose the correct word:

site / sight
He lost his _____ when he was ten.
This is the _____ of the new building.

right / write
I'll _____ to thank her for the present.
It's not _____ to simply ignore her.

knight / night
I slept so badly last _____.
A _____ used to wear heavy armour.

YEAR 4   WEEKS 21-30
50 Word Revision List

square	squeeze	relax
orphan	sphere	fright
glisten	bizarre	galaxy
whistle	queue	moisten
crumb	whinny	doubt
fasten	squash	hazel
physical	array	yacht
sight	squirrel	destroy
knob	height	triumph
betray	frieze	whisker
answer	quarrel	tranquil
knelt	purity	knock
queasy	whereas	photograph
thigh	quantity	island
wheat	misery	knight
beauty	conquer	column
phrase		family

Complete Graded Spelling Lists with Spelling and Vocabulary Exercises

YEAR 4 LIST 31

ought
bought
fought
nought
sought
thought
brought
dough
though
although
bough
plough
drought
cough
rough
tough
enough
through

EXTRA WORDS

trough
thoughtless
thoughtful
thoughtfully
thoughtfulness

1. Find the List 31 word that means:

nothing _____
should _____
sufficient _____
branch _____
hunted _____
harsh _____
clashed _____

2. Choose the correct word:

bought / brought
bought - past of *buy*
brought - past of *bring*

We _____ eggs at the shop on the corner.
We _____ our friends along with us.

3. Choose the correct word:

bow / bough
There is a parrot on the _____ above you.
They _____ their heads to the king.

fort / fought
For years, this country _____ a war.
An old _____ sits on the headland.

sort / sought
He _____ a job in my company.
What _____ of pasta do you prefer?

rough / ruff
He wore a shirt with a _____ at the cuffs.
The sea was very _____ today.

through / threw
I _____ the bag in the rubbish bin.
She came rushing _____ the door.

4. Find the List 31 word rhyming with:

off _____
out _____
crew _____

YEAR 4 LIST 32

- wrap
- wrath
- wreath
- wren
- wreck
- wrench
- wretch
- write
- wrote
- written
- wring
- wrist
- wrong
- wrung
- wrangle
- wrestle
- wriggle
- wrinkle

EXTRA WORDS

- wry
- wrathful
- wrongful
- wriggling
- wrinkling

1. Match the words to their meaning:

wreck wreath wrench wrath wrangle wring

leaves arranged in a ring
_____

a quarrel, angry dispute
_____

intense anger
_____

to pull suddenly
_____

a twist a thing tightly
_____

a thing completely destroyed _____

2. Find three related List 32 words:

_____
_____
_____

3. Find the List 32 word that means:

crinkle _____
grapple _____
squirm _____

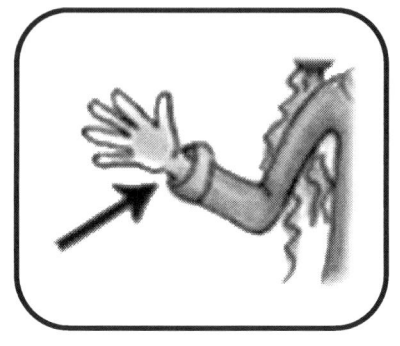

4. Choose the correct word:

ring / wring
What a lovely _____!
I'll _____ out the shirt and hang it up.

rung / wrung
I've _____ my aunt twice today.
I could've _____ his neck for being so mean.

rote / wrote
I _____ to my penpal.
I learnt the verbs by _____, so that I wouldn't forget them.

retch / wretch
The poor _____ was living on the streets.
The vile smell was making us _____.

rap / wrap
Did you hear a _____ at the door?
I'll _____ up her birthday present.

Complete Graded Spelling Lists with Spelling and Vocabulary Exercises

YEAR 4 LIST 33

dove
glove
shove
above
cover
lovely
honey
money
monk
monkey
month
oven
dozen
blood
flood
front
comfort
company

EXTRA WORDS

shovel
smother
lovelier
loveliest
loveliness

3. Match the List 33 word to its opposite:

below or _____

back or _____

nun or _____

4. Find the List 33 word related to:

monetary _____

loveliness _____

frontier _____

companion _____

uncomfortable _____

1. Find the List 33 noun that fits best:

_____ on a hand

_____ of actors

_____ in an abbey

_____ of water

_____ in the bank

_____ of the year

_____ in your veins

2. Find the List 33 word rhyming with:

blunt _____

hunk _____

cousin _____

govern _____

5. Look at these:

key + ~ed = keyed
volley + ~ed = volleyed

Now try these:

money + ~ed = _____

honey + ~ed = _____

monkey + ~ed = _____

Complete Graded Spelling Lists with Spelling and Vocabulary Exercises

YEAR 4 LIST 34

wad
wan
waft
wand
wash
wasp
war
ward
warn
wart
water
watch
waltz
wander
wardrobe
warrior
dwarf
thwart

EXTRA WORDS

wanly
warden
watery
watchful
dwarfed

1. Find the List 34 word rhyming with:

ponder _____
porter _____
slosh   _____
odd   _____
faun   _____

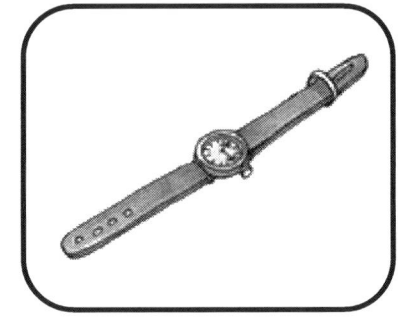

2. Match the word to its meaning:

wan thwart ward
wad waft waltz

zone, area   _____
pale, weak   _____
drift, float _____
stop, spoil _____
lump, mass   _____
a dance   _____

3. Choose the correct word:

war / wore
The _____ was a tragedy for the people.
I _____ my best clothes to the party.

warn / worn
I've never _____ earrings before.
I'd better _____ her about the traffic.

4. Place the correct word in the sentence:

watch watched watchful
watchfulness watchable
unwatched unwatchable

We _____ the race with excitement.
She was _____, and so she saw it first.
The film was so bad, we found it _____.

5. Find the List 34 words with two meanings:

_____ out for him in the crowd.
    - and -
My _____ no longer tells the correct time.

* * *

He's in the children's _____ in the hospital.
    - and -
The brooch is meant to _____ of evil spirits.

94

Complete Graded Spelling Lists with Spelling and Vocabulary Exercises

YEAR 4 LIST 35

swab
swan
swap
swat
swarm
swamp
word
work
worm
world
worse
worst
worship
worthy
wonder
worry
woman
women

3. Find the List 35 noun that fits best:

a man and a _____
a _____ of bees
an earth _____
men and _____
a _____ and a cygnet
a compound _____
a fly _____

1. Find the List 35 word rhyming with:

terse _____
term _____
hurry _____
stop _____
quirk _____

4. Choose the correct word:

wander / wonder
wander - walk aimlessly
wonder - question

He'll _____ what's happened to us.
I like to _____ along the beach.

worst / wurst
worst - most bad
wurst - a sausage

This is the _____ book I have ever read.
We ate our bread with _____.

worse / worst
worse - more bad
worst - most bad

The weather is much _____ than before.
It was the _____ day of my life.

2. Look at these:

swab + ~ed = swa**bb**ed
swab + ~ing = swa**bb**ing

Now try these:

swap + ~ed = _____

swap + ~ing = _____

swat + ~ed = _____

swat + ~ing = _____

EXTRA WORDS

worthier
worthiest
worsen
worsened
worsening

YEAR 4 LIST 36

meow
bower
cower
power
tower
flower
shower
powder
dowdy
rowdy
downy
dowry
drowsy
bowel
vowel
towel
trowel
prowess

EXTRA WORDS

rowdier
dowdiest
flowery
drowsily
empowered

1. Find the List 36 noun that means:

sleepy _____
boisterous _____
strength _____

2. Choose the correct word:

flour / flower

You need two cups of _____ for a cake.
He gave me a pretty _____.

3. Match the words to their meaning:

prowess bower cower dowdy downy dowry trowel

drab, outdated
_____

soft and fluffy
_____

money paid to a groom
_____

to hide or shrink away
_____

ability, evident skill
_____

a small gardening spade
_____

a nook or dell of plants
_____

4. Find the List 36 noun that fits best:

talcum _____
a hot _____
a cat's _____
consonant or _____
a bride's _____
a castle's _____

5. Look at these:

downy + ~*er* = down*ier*
downy + ~*est* = down*iest*

Now try these:

rowdy + ~*er* = _____

rowdy + ~*est* = _____

dowdy + ~*er* = _____

dowdy + ~*est* = _____

Complete Graded Spelling Lists with Spelling and Vocabulary Exercises

YEAR 4 LIST 37

guffaw
jigsaw
mildew
curfew
askew
nephew
cashew
allow
endow
elbow
widow
shadow
meadow
window
bungalow
bestow
wallow
swallow

EXTRA WORDS

shadowy
swallowed
bestowal
allowance
endowment

1. Add ~*ew* or ~*ow* to make a List 37 word:

end ~ _____
mild ~ _____
wall ~ _____
ask ~ _____
best ~ _____

2. What am I? Find the List 37 noun:

I am a nut: _____

I am part of your arm: _____

I follow you around: _____

My husband has died: _____

Cows graze on me: _____

I am your sibling's son: _____

3. Find the List 37 word with two meanings:

A _____ has made its nest in our tree.
   - and -
Do not _____ the toothpaste.

* * *

I could see her waving through the _____.
   - and -
There was only a small _____ of opportunity for landing the rocket.

4. Match the words to their meaning:

mildew guffaw bestow wallow curfew askew bungalow

a loud, throaty laugh _____

wonky, not straight _____

to roll or lie in water or mud _____

large single-storey house _____

to give or donate _____

a fine, white mould _____

a deadline for returning home _____

97

Complete Graded Spelling Lists with Spelling and Vocabulary Exercises

YEAR 4 LIST 38

daily
dairy
fairy
daisy
afraid
mermaid
detail
obtain
curtain
fountain
maintain
mountain
entertain
campaign
affair
despair
repair
portrait

EXTRA WORDS

prairie
villain
sustain
mountainous
villainous

1. Find the List 38 word rhyming with:

irate _____
stale _____
scaly _____
hazy _____

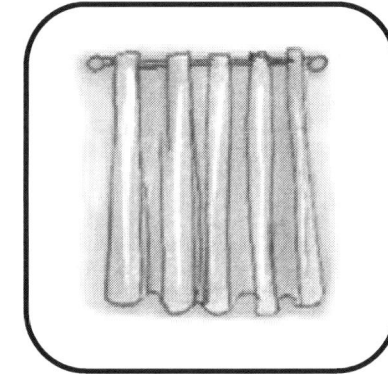

2. Choose the correct word:

dairy / diary

She records the events of a day in a _____.
The cows are milked in the _____.

3. What am I? Find the List 38 noun:

I am a tiny person:
_____

I spout water:
_____

I am very large:
_____

I cover a window:
_____

I'm good at swimming:
_____

I house cows:
_____

I am a flower:
_____

4. Find the List 38 word related to:

reparation _____
portray _____
day _____
maintenance _____
desperation _____
font _____

5. Place the correct word in the sentence:

**entertain entertained
entertaining
entertainingly
entertainer
entertainment**

The singer was _____.

The singer was a true _____.

I was impressed by the _____ provided by the singer.

Complete Graded Spelling Lists with Spelling and Vocabulary Exercises

YEAR 4 LIST 39

eager
beaker
sneaker
steamer
streamer
beaver
beacon
reason
season
treason
weary
dreary
sweater
feather
heather
leather
weather
weapon

3. Find the List 39 word with two meanings:

I always _____ the gravy with soy sauce.
- and -
Spring is the _____ for new growth.

1. Add List 39 words to the table:

Noun	Adjective
_____	seasonal
eagerness	_____
_____	reasonable
_____	weathered
dreariness	_____
_____	leathery

4. Look at these:

wary + ~*ly* = war<u>i</u>ly
wary + ~*ness* = war<u>i</u>ness

Now try these:

weary + ~*ly* = _____

weary + ~*ness* = _____

dreary + ~*ly* = _____

dreary + ~*ness* = _____

2. Match the word to its meaning:

**treason steamer
beaker beacon eager
dreary heather**

a boat powered by steam _____

disloyalty to a ruler _____

a light used as a signal _____

a plant with purple flowers _____

a flat-bottomed jug _____

lifeless _____

keen _____

5. Choose the correct word:

weather / whether

I don't know _____ to go out today.
Let's find out _____ it will be sunny.
Let's listen to the _____ report.

EXTRA WORDS

bleary
cleaver
measles
wearily
drearily

YEAR 4 LIST 40

fierce
pierce
belief
relief
mischief
glacier
soldier
courier
cashier
frontier
sieve
grieve
achieve
believe
relieve
reprieve
retrieve
handkerchief

EXTRA WORDS

piercing
sieving
believing
grievous
mischievous

1. Add ~*ier* or ~*ieve* to make a List 40 word:

repr ~ _____
bel ~ _____
cour ~ _____
retr ~ _____
glac ~ _____

2. Find the List 40 word that means:

fighter _____
prick _____
trouble _____
mourn _____
vicious _____
border _____
pardon _____

3. Place the correct word in the sentence:

belief believe believer
believable believably
unbelievable
unbelievably

I have no _____ in his claims.
I can't _____ his claims.
His claims are simply not _____.

4. Add the same word twice to each sentence, to make two mnemonics:

- Sol____rs often _____ in battle.
- Beware of the _____ in your be____fs.

5. Look at these:

sieve → sieving
believe → believable
grief → grievous

Now try these:

achieve + ~*ing* =
_____
achieve + ~*able* =
_____
retrieve + ~*ing* =
_____
retrieve + ~*able* =
_____
mischief + ~*ous* =
_____

YEAR 4   WEEKS 31-40
50 Word Revision List

powder	fountain	wrong
feather	window	enough
believe	meadow	blood
warrior	women	monkey
shower	glacier	wrestle
mermaid	written	despair
swallow	worry	mountain
oven	vowel	achieve
campaign	comfort	money
swap	dreary	through
wreath	world	weather
reason	mischief	above
shadow	fought	nephew
beacon	water	soldier
front	though	towel
flower	worst	brought
cough		entertain

YEAR 4 LIST 41

heir
rein
vein
reign
feign
foreign
sovereign
conceive
deceive
perceive
receive
conceit
either
neither
seize
seizure
weir
weird

EXTRA WORDS

sheikh
skein
heist
feisty
protein

1. Match the word to its meaning:

weir conceive conceit feign sovereign perceive

to pretend _____

pride, vanity
_____

a low dam in a river
_____

supreme, dominant
_____

to bring into life
_____

to see or observe
_____

2. Find the List 41 word rhyming with:

bear _____
trees _____
treat _____
beard _____

3. Complete the table:

Verb	Noun
_____	deception
_____	perception
conceive	_____
receive	_____

4. Choose the correct word:

air / heir

The _____ is fresh.
The _____ is too young to be king.

seas / seize

You must _____ the handle very firmly.
The _____ are rough.

rein / reign
rein - on a horse
reign - of a ruler

I held the _____ tightly in my hand.
The queen's _____ lasted for seventy years.

vain / vein
vain - overly proud
vein - blood vessel

You can see a _____ through your skin.
some actors appear to be very _____.

YEAR 4 LIST 42

build
guild
built
guilt
guide
guile
guise
disguise
suit
fruit
juice
bruise
cruise
biscuit
circuit
pursuit
recruit
suite

EXTRA WORDS

juicy
fruity
guilty
guiding
beguiling

2. Find the List 42 noun that fits best:

innocence or _____
a business _____
_____ and vegetables
_____ of a lemon
an electrical _____

3. Find the List 42 word with two meanings:

It is a formal dinner, so wear a _____ and tie.
- and -
This dress does not _____ me at all.

4. Match the word to its meaning:

**guild guile suite guise
circuit recruit pursuit**

hunt, chase _____
set of rooms _____
circular path _____
trainee, new member
_____
trickery, subterfuge
_____
appearance, facade
_____
society, association
_____

1. Choose the correct word:

crews / cruise

I went on a _____ around the world.
There were _____ came to put out the fire.

brews / bruise

He _____ his own beer.
I have a _____ from hitting my knee.

suite / sweet

We booked a _____ of rooms.
I don't like my tea to be too _____.

gilt / guilt
gilt - covered in gold
guilt - being at fault

His _____ about hurting his friend was hard to bear.
The painting has a _____ frame.

Complete Graded Spelling Lists with Spelling and Vocabulary Exercises

YEAR 4 LIST 43

abroad
alarm
alert
amend
amount
amuse
await
award
aware
adapt
adopt
adore
adhere
admit
adjust
advance
advice
advise

EXTRA WORDS

abide
align
amass
adept
adverse

1. Find the List 43 word that rhymes with:

appear _____
stopped _____
opened _____
eyes _____
bored _____
bruise _____

2. Find the List 43 word that fits best:

to _____ an orphan

to _____ guilt

to _____ a prize

to _____ a dial

to travel _____

3. Choose the correct word:

advice / advise
advice - is a noun
advise - is a verb

The best _____ is always given for free.
I don't know what to _____ you to do.
I don't think she will follow his _____.

4. Look at this:

apart + ~*ment* = apartment
refine + ~*ment* = refinement

Now try these:

adjust + ~*ment* =
_____

advance + ~*ment* =
_____

amuse + ~*ment* =
_____

5. Add List 43 words to the table:

Verb	Noun
_____	admission
_____	adherence
_____	awareness
_____	adoration
_____	advice

Complete Graded Spelling Lists with Spelling and Vocabulary Exercises

YEAR 4 LIST 44

combine
compare
compel
compute
conceal
concept
concern
conclude
conduct
confess
confide
confine
confirm
conform
confuse
consist
contain
convict

3. Add *con~* or *com~* to make a List 44 word:

~ fide _____
~ pel _____
~ firm _____
~ pare _____
~ bine _____

1. Find the List 44 word closest in meaning to:

force _____
idea _____
admit _____
behaviour _____
fear, worry _____
hide, mask _____

4. Find the List 44 word rhyming with:

brood _____
news _____
earn _____
stepped _____
fair _____

2. Look at this:

express → expression
infuse → infusion
exclude → exclusion

Now try these:

confuse + ~*ion* = _____

confess + ~*ion* = _____

conclude + ~*ion* = _____

5. Look at this:

predict → prediction
except → exception
reform → reformation

Now try these:

convict + ~*ion* = _____

concept + ~*ion* = _____

confirm + ~*ion* = _____

EXTRA WORDS

conspire
comprise
contort
converse
computer

Complete Graded Spelling Lists with Spelling and Vocabulary Exercises

YEAR 4 LIST 45

decide
declare
deduce
deduct
defeat
defer
define
deliver
depart
depose
describe
devote
discover
discuss
disease
disgust
dismiss
dispute

EXTRA WORDS

derive
detain
discord
dispel
disrupt

1. Add de~ or dis~ to make a List 45 word:

~ fer _____
~ duct _____
~ gust _____
~ pute _____
~ liver _____

2. Find the List 45 word rhyming with:

complete _____
knows _____
shoot _____
repair _____
afloat _____

3. Word maths:

discuss + ~ion =
_____

devote + ~ion =
_____

deduct + ~ion =
_____

declare + ~ion =
_____

4. Match the word to its meaning:

devote defer depose disgust dismiss define

to make clear, outline
_____

to put off, postpone
_____

to give yourself to
_____

to remove, overthrow
_____

revulsion, distaste
_____

to send away
_____

5. Choose the correct word:

disgust / discussed

We _____ what to do about her car. On her face was a look of pure _____.

Complete Graded Spelling Lists with Spelling and Vocabulary Exercises

Oh my goodness!!

3. Match the List 46 word to its opposite:

import or export
include or exclude
inform or misinform

YEAR 4 LIST 46

exceed
excel
except
excite
exclaim
excuse
exile
express
extend
import
impose
impress
include
inflame
inform
insist
instruct
inverse

1. Add *ex~* or *in~* to make a List 46 word:

~ sist   _ex_
~ cuse   _ex_
~ form   _in_
~ struct   _in_
~ cel   _ex_

4. Find the List 46 word that rhymes with:

flight   _excite_
flows   _impose_
rehearse   _inverse_
leapt   _except_
stampede   _exceed_
plucked   _instruct_

2. Word maths:

express + ~*ion* = _expression_
except + ~*ion* = _exception_
instruct + ~*ion* = _instruction_
inverse + ~*ion* = _inversion_
include + ~*ion* = _includion_

5. Choose the correct word:

accept / except
accept - to agree
except - apart from

I cannot _accept_ that he is really gone.
I'll buy everything _except_ the drinks.
We should _accept_ their offer of help.

EXTRA WORDS

exchange
impart
incite
infuse
insure

Complete Graded Spelling Lists with Spelling and Vocabulary Exercises

YEAR 4 LIST 47

persist
pervade
precise
preclude
predict
prefer
prelude
prepare
present
presence
prevail
preview
proclaim
product
profess
promote
provide
provoke

EXTRA WORDS

prediction
production
profession
promotion
presentation

1. Add *pre~* or *pro~* to make a List 47 word:

~ vail _____
~ mote _____
~ lude _____
~ fess _____
~ voke _____

2. Choose the correct word:

presents / presence

Did you get _____ for your birthday?
Her _____ made it hard to concentrate.

3. Match the word to its meaning:

prelude profess
proclaim prevail
provoke pervade

to triumph _____
to cause _____
to claim _____
something coming before _____
to spread across _____
to announce publicly _____

4. Word maths:

predict + ~*ion* = _____

promote + ~*ion* = _____

precise + ~*ion* = _____

prepare + ~*ion* = _____

proclaim + ~*ion* = _____

5. The prefix *pre~* often means *before*. Find the List 47 word that means:

to forecast: _____
something prior to a later event: _____
to get ready in advance: _____
to see something in advance: _____

Complete Graded Spelling Lists with Spelling and Vocabulary Exercises

YEAR 4 LIST 48

recite
record
recoil
reduce
refine
refuse
regret
remind
remote
repeat
repent
reply
report
resist
respond
restrain
result
reveal

EXTRA WORDS

relay
repeal
retain
return
review

---

3. Find the List 48 word that rhymes with:

insane _____
gloat _____
discrete _____
insight _____
scored _____

4. Find the List 48 verb that fits best:

to _____ a secret

to _____ a poem

to _____ in horror

to _____ someone of an appointment

to _____ a crime to the police

5. Add List 48 words to the table:

Verb	Noun
_____	repetition
_____	revelation
_____	reduction
_____	recitation

---

1. Match the word to its meaning:

recoil recite remote
refine restrain repent

to regret, apologize
_____

to pull back, flinch
_____

to make finer
_____

distant, isolated
_____

to narrate, perform
_____

to hold back, detain
_____

2. Find the List 48 word that can be spoken in two ways:

It's not my fault, so I _____ to say sorry.
- and -
Bags of _____ were piled in the street.

109

Complete Graded Spelling Lists with Spelling and Vocabulary Exercises

YEAR 4 LIST 49

Monday
Tuesday
Wednesday
Thursday
Friday
Saturday
Sunday
today
tomorrow
yesterday
first
second
third
fourth
fifth
eighth
primary
secondary

EXTRA WORDS

eleventh
twelfth
twentieth
thirtieth
fortieth

1. Choose the correct word:

forth / fourth

We set _____ from our house on foot.
It was the _____ time I'd seen the film.

2. Place the correct word in the sentence:

**prime   primer
primary   primarily
primate   primitive**

Red and yellow are both _____ colours.
He is _____ an artist.
The people lived in very _____ houses.
An ape is a _____.

3. Write the words in full, in alphabetical order:

**Sat Thur Tue
Mon Fri Wed**

_____   _____
_____   _____
_____   _____

4. Write these List 49 words in numerical order:

5th 2nd 8th 4th 1st 3rd

_____   _____
_____   _____
_____   _____

5. Find the List 49 words with two meanings:

I will be with you in just a _____.
- and -
I was disappointed to have come _____.

* * *

We go to school at the local _____ school.
- and -
My _____ concern was to keep her safe.

Complete Graded Spelling Lists with Spelling and Vocabulary Exercises

YEAR 4 LIST 50

January
February
March
April
May
June
July
August
September
October
November
December
spring
summer
autumn
winter
morning
evening

3. Complete the table of nouns:

autumn November
August evening
December winter

Common	Proper
_____	_____
_____	_____
_____	_____

1. Find the List 50 word that fits best:

I go to bed in the _____.

I wake in the _____.

I like the _____ because it is hot.

I like the _____ because it is cold.

I like to play in the leaves in the _____.

I like watching the birds nesting in the _____.

My birthday is in _____.

4. Choose the correct word:

morning / mourning

The next _____, the bird made its nest.
She is in _____, because her aunt died.

5. Find the List 50 word that rhymes with:

prey _____

awning _____

balloon _____

imply _____

plumber _____

2. Find the List 50 word with two meanings:

A _____ in the bed is digging into me.
- and -
These birds fly north in the _____.

EXTRA WORDS

afternoon
fortnight
midday
holiday
birthday

YEAR 4   WEEKS 41-50
50 Word Revision List

exclaim	except	Wednesday
Tuesday	impress	reign
adjust	confuse	November
presence	disgust	advise
tomorrow	prepare	autumn
February	conceal	heir
seize	inflame	circuit
compel	Saturday	secondary
describe	exceed	January
repeat	provoke	defeat
preview	cruise	guide
first	juice	concept
adhere	disease	recoil
respond	advance	excite
August	disguise	weird
perceive	foreign	fruit
either		discover

Complete Graded Spelling Lists with Spelling and Vocabulary Exercises

ANSWERS

Year Three

List 1: 1. nerve, carve, serve, starve, swerve; 2. smart, swerve, spark, sparse, serve, nerve; 3. start, smart, sparse, starve, serve; 4. stark, terse, snarl, swerve, nerve, sparse

List 2: 1. haste, halve, tense, sense, dense, taste; 2. rinse, baste, solve, taste; 3. haste, sense, dense, baste, paste; 4. cents, sense; tense, tents; waist, waste, waste

List 3: 1. gleam, grease, steam, please, dream; 2. gleam, cease, grease, lease, smear; 3. steel, steal; 4. peace, clean, clear, please; 5. ceased, ceasing, greased, greasing, pleased, pleasing

List 4: 1. least, feast, beast, east, treat; 2. creak, creek; cheap, cheep; 3. feast, freak, sneak, yeast, bleak; 4. least, speak, freak, east, sheath; 5. stealing, stolen, stole

List 5: 1. weave, breathe, meant, leant; 2. death, leave, dead, breadth, bread, deaf; 3. deafen, deafening, deaden, deadening; 4. dead, death; breath, breathe; 5. leant, lent; bred, bread

List 6: 1. stank, stink; drank, drink; 2. flank, crank, clink, brink, slang, clamp; 3. blank, plank, drink, blink, cramp; 4. stamp, stamp; 5. stamp, slang, crank, clamp, stank

List 7: 1. grandest, grandly, grand, grandeur; 2. stand, stand, stand; trunk, trunk, trunk; 3. slung, clung, brand, grand, flung, gland; 4. clung, swung, flung, slung, stand, twist

List 8: 1. sting, frost, sling, cling, frond, blond; 2. sting, trust, fling, bring; 3. trust, sting, fling, crust, cling, swing; 4. blunt, scold, frond, prong, stunt, crimp

List 9: 1. stump, blend, slump, spend, plump; 2. crept, spent, swept, dwelt, slept, slump; 3. crest, crest; 4. sleepier, sleepless, sleepily; 5. stump, trend, spasm, clump, prism, blend

List 10: 1. print, pant, flint, glint, slant, grant; 2. flask, plant, blast, print, clasp, glint; 3. grant, flask, flint, slant, glint, clasp; 4. craft, craft; plant, plant

List 11: 1. ready, heavy, health, wealth, thread, heart, swear, wear; 2. tear, tear; 3. ready, stealth, threat, steady, tear, wear; 4. where, wear; bare, bear; pear, pair

List 12: 1. break, search, earth, pearl, great, yearn; 2. great, early, coarse, broad, heard; 3. earn, break, great, board, heard, hoarse, coarse; 4. bored, board; great, grate

List 13: 1. oath, poach, foal, croak, gloat, coal; 2. groan, grown; 3. roast, gloat, toast, throat, float; 4. croaking, cloaked, toaster, coastal, goalless, boastful, throatiest; 5. coast, coast

List 14: 1. stairs, flair, braid, claim; 2. wail, whale; plain, plane; stairs, stares; 3. snail, stain, drain, vain, frail, plain; 4. frail, claim, drain, grain, vain, bail

List 15: 1. saint, moist, noise, praise; 2. waist, waste; praise, prays; 3. spoil, waist, trait, moist, hoist, faith; 4. hoist, spoil, saint, trait, waist, moist; 5. faint, faint

List 16: 1. charge, grudge, large, smudge, judge, nudge; 2. stage, stage; charge, charge; change, change; 3. large, judge, orange, fudge; 4. smudge, grudge, budge, cadge, nudge, trudge

List 17: 1. cringe, twinge, ridge, binge, bridge; 2. lounge, lunge, purge, ridge, singe, twinge; 3. singed, lunged, lounging, bridging, surging; 4. bridge, lounge, twinge, hinge, singe, bulge

List 18: 1. lodge, lodge; gorge, gorge; 2. spongy, pledging, lodger, forgery, dislodged, divergent, emerging; 3. ledge, forge, wedge, hedge, gorge; 4. verge, pledge, dredge, wedge, scourge, dodge

List 19: 1. daze, days; lays, laze; doze, dose; pries, prize; 2. blaze, froze, craze, maze; 3. blaze, glaze, haze, craze, raze, faze; 4. dozy, hazy, crazy, jazzy

List 20: 1. quell, quota, quest, quash, qualm, quail; 2. quiet, quake, quilt, quench, quell, quoit, quest; 3. quest, quite, quail, quake, qualm, quash, quote; 4. quill, quill

List 21: 1. striding, splitting, stroking, straining, strapping, striving; 2. stride, straw, strain, stroll, stroke, stray; 3. splint, split, strike, strip, stripe, stroll; 4. stray, street, straw, stroke

List 22: 1. screw, screen, spray, sprig, scrap; 2. scripture, script, prescription; 3. spread, sprout, screw, scrum, scroll, spray; 4. spread, spree, screw, sprain, screen, scream; 5. scrub, scrub

List 23: 1. streak, stress, strait, stream; 2. strength, strengthen, strongest, strongly; 3. string, string; 4. stress, stuck, stream, ditch, length, fetch; 5. fetch, itch, length, notch, strength, stretch

List 24: 1. clutch, snatch, switch, match, stitch; 2. latch, scratch, thatch, stitch, pitch, sketch; 3. scratch, thatch, stitch, snatch, switch; 4. match, match; hatch, hatch; 5. which, witch

List 25: 1. drench, clench, hunch, trench, flinch, winch; 2. bunch, pinch, clench, lunch, trench, bench; 3. punch, drench, crunch, clench, trench; 4. crunches, flinches, hunches, benches, belches

List 26: 1. glitter, scatter, splatter, twitter, clatter; 2. shattered, littering, splattered, battering; 3. batter, batter; letter, letter; matter, matter; 4. better, latter, bitter, litter, letter, shatter, twitter

List 27: 1. udder, splutter, rudder, stutter, shudder, clutter; 2. butter, rubber, rudder, udder, flutter, gutter, shutter; 3. blubber, stutter, flutter, rubber, shutter; 4. utter, utter; blubber, blubber

List 28: 1. inner, dinner, stopper, manner, suffer; 2. differed, difference, differ, different; 3. flipper, pepper, banner, supper, manner; 4. suffered, suffering; stammered, stammering; 5. zipper, slipper, flipper, stopper

List 29: 1. following, narrowly, sorrowful, borrower, shallowest; 2. burrow, bellow, hollow, sorrow, fellow; 3. burrow, barrow, pillow, arrow; 4. sorrow, narrow, borrow, shallow, follow; 5. allowed, disallowed, allowance

List 30: 1. happening, summoned, suddenly, commoner, unbuttoned; 2. commonly, commonest, commoner; 3. sudden, possum, ribbon, happen; 4. common, summon, sudden, sullen, ribbon, happen; 5. bottom, bottom; blossom, blossom

List 31: 1. funnel, carrot, parrot, tunnel, flannel; 2. funnelled, funnelling, channelled, channelling; 3. puppet, ballot, nugget, bullet, kennel, summit, rabbit; 4. channel, channel; barrel, barrel; parrot, parrot

List 32: 1. thief, niece, grief, piece, brief; 2. pier, peer; tier, tear; peace, piece; 3. niece, friend, priest, brief, piece, chief, pier; 4. piece, pie; end, friend

List 33: 1. mouse, sound, proud; 2. pound, pound; ground, ground; bound, bound; 3. mound, shroud, ground, proud, cloud, hound; 4. flour, flower; 5. found, wound, bound, ground, scour

Complete Graded Spelling Lists with Spelling and Vocabulary Exercises

Year Three, cont/...

List 34: 1. south, stout, shout, spout, count, mount, trout; 2. snout, joust, pouch, crouch, stout, scout, stout; 3. couch, spout, trout, crouch, snout; 4. count, count; mouth, mouth

List 35: 1. source, course, pounce; 2. trouble, touch; group, youth; course, source; soul, mould; 3. doubled, bouncer, troubling, soulless, resourceful; 4. soul, sole; course, coarse; source, sauce

List 36: 1. aunt, taut, cause, faun, sauce, launch; 2. mall, maul; paws, pause; haul, hall; 3. cause, clause, sauce; 4. aunt, taut, clause; 5. sauce, taut, faun, aunt

List 37: 1. cruel, lion, fluid, neon, alien, poem, duet; 2. idea, alien, poem, create; 3. duel, dual; lyre, liar; 4. ruin, poem, cruel, fluid, riot, diet, idea

List 38: 1. bubbly, wiggly, giggly, wobbly; 2. baffle, rubble, scuffle, babble, ruffle, hobble; 3. hobble, wobble, wiggle, bubble, scribble, giggle; 4. wiggle, nibble, scribble, raffle, bubble, babble

List 39: 1. puddle, settle, huddle, kettle, cuddle; 2. saddle, saddle; fiddle, fiddle; 3. settler, huddled, cuddy, rattling; 4. cattle, riddle, battle, kettle, rattle, bottle; 5. settlement, settling, unsettling

List 40: 1. grizzle, tussle, hassle, muzzle, drizzle; 2. supple, tussle, muzzle, topple, nuzzle, grapple; 3. hassle, ripple, nozzle, puzzle, dazzle; 4. cripple, grizzle, nuzzle, puzzle, sizzle, topple

List 41: 1. marries, married, rallies, rallied, ferries, ferried; 2. jelly, curry, jolly, silly, sorry, rally; 3. fairy, ferry; berry, bury; 4. silly, jolly, sorry, marry, merry, hurry

List 42: 1. ditty, tatty, buddy, giddy, pretty; 2. happy, buddy, funny, tatty, ditty, hobby, giddy; 3. prettier, prettiest, funnier, funniest, choppier, choppiest; 4. mummy, mummy; dummy, dummy

List 43: 1. truly, lily, pity, lady, study, baby; 2. fancy, fancy; body, body; 3. holy, wholly; 4. study, lady, body, duty, pity; 5. merciful, plentiful, pitiful, fanciful, dutiful

List 44: 1. bury, navy, busy, puny, pony; 2. berry, bury; storey, story; 3. glory, puny, cosy, fury, wary, tiny, rosy; 4. various, glorious, furious, business, wariness, cosiness

List 45: 1. monster, pester, enter, mister, splinter, plaster; 2. fester, pester, foster, cluster, roster, banter; 3. master, sister, enter, canter; 4. plaster, foster, cluster, roster, splinter, blister

List 46: 1. shaker, grater, player, oyster, choker, garter; 2. shaker, layer, neuter, later, cater; 3. cater, baker, porter, player; 4. neuter, porter, prayer, foyer, oyster; 5. grater, greater

List 47: 1. slanderous, ponderous, thunderous, murderous; 2. boarder, border; 3. murder, partner, plunder, slender, spider, thunder; 4. partner, boarder, slender; 5. ponder, plunder, girder, blunder, tinder, slander, former

List 48: 1. hunger, clever, tiger, hover; 2. finger, clever, danger, tiger, silver, hunger; 3. linger, sever, hover, fever, shiver, clever; 4. ginger, hover, linger, liver, sever, silver

List 49: 1. prosper, proper, temper, number, viper; 2. timber, prosper, hamper, tamper, scamper, viper, slumber; 3. clamber, slumber, scamper, prosper; 4. number, member, paper, wiper; 5. hamper, hamper

List 50: 1. no-one, wherever; 2. whereas, whereabouts, nowhere, everywhere; 3. forever, whether, someone, nowhere, whoever, somewhere; 4. therefore, otherwise, meanwhile, anyway; 5. otherwise, anyway, therefore, whoever, meanwhile, no-one

Year Four

List 1: 1. forty, thirty, twenty, twelve, eleven, fifty; 2. forty, twenty, fourteen; 3. nineteen, thousand, seventeen, eleven, twenty, fifty; 4. fifteen, twenty-one, eighteen, thirty, forty, fourteen, thousand

List 2: 1. stable, nimble, humble, stumble, bible; 2. crumble, crumble; scramble, scramble; 3. tremble, stumble, mumble, gamble; 4. noble, fable, tremble, nimble, humble, stable; 5. unable, able, disability

List 3: 1. people; 2. tripling, kindling, sampling; 3. staple, staple; handle, handle; 4. simple, triple, needle, candle, steeple, cradle, people; 5. temple, sample, fondle, bundle, kindle, triple, ample

List 4: 1. gurgle, bustle, rustle; 2. turtle, beetle, bangle, tangle, castle, title; 3. single, bustle, turtle, burgle, startle; 4. title, title; 5. tangle, title, angle, single, burgle, strangle

List 5: 1. trickle, sprinkle, twinkle, sparkle, chuckle, freckle, crackle; 2. trifle, trifle; buckle, buckle; 3. fickle, prickle, twinkle, sprinkle, trickle; 4. prickle, crackle. buckle, sparkle, ankle, shackle

List 6: 1. rocket, locket, jacket, bucket, pocket; 2. packet, ticket, wicker, socket, sticker; 3. cricket, sticker, bucket, bicker, thicket; 4. bracketed, ticketed, bickered, rocketed, reckoned; 5. racquet, racket

List 7: 1. racquet; basket, cadet, toilet, helmet; 2. carpeting, trumpeting, blanketing, targeting; 3. blanket, blanket; 4. velvet, helmet, closet, cadet, secret; 5. magnetic, secretive, velveteen, trumpeter, toiletries, forgetful

List 8: 1. organ, human, orbit, permit, credit, limit; 2. digit, digit; organ, organ; 3. edit, turban, permit, human, spirit; 4. habit, pivot, merit; 5. limited, limiting; orbited, orbiting

List 9: 1. raven, raisin, heaven, siren, napkin; 2. heaven, burden, haven, napkin, siren, open; 3. heaven, kitchen, napkin, pumpkin, raisin, raven; 4. garden, kitchen, pumpkin, violin, raven

List 10: 1. dragon, canyon, pardon, crimson, crayon; 2. cannon, wagon, iron, apron, crayon, pardon; 3. nylon, salon, demon, canyon, baton, icon; 4. iconic, demonize, wagoner, ironing, personality

List 11: 1. random, freedom, tantrum, pilgrim, problem; 2. ransom, seldom, custom, emblem, tantrum, problem, random; 3. wisest, wisely, wisdom, wiser; 4. wisdom, freedom, venom, problem, emblem, custom

List 12: 1. subvert, insert, superb, expert, concert, convert; 2. assert, insert, subvert, convert, govern; 3. overt, pattern, convert, inert, cavern; 4. proverb, overt, convert, covert, subvert, assert

List 13: 1. sacred, period, bishop; 2. rugged, motif, dogged, ragged, kindred, serif; 3. bishop, tulip, turnip, crooked, sacred; 4. hatred, crooked, wicked, ragged, gallop; 5. period, method, sacred

List 14: 1. public, toxic, basic, ethic; 2. critic, topic, ethical, comical; 3. critical, criticize, critically, criticism; 4. comic, basic, panic, frolic, attic, hectic; 5. basic, toxic, comic, sonic

Complete Graded Spelling Lists with Spelling and Vocabulary Exercises

Year Four, cont/...

List 15: 1. valid, validate, validity; 2. rigid, timid, lucidity, stupidity, acidity; 3. lucid, valid, solid, placid; 4. stupid, rapid, humid, vivid; 5. livid, rigid, putrid, lucid, morbid, placid

List 16: 1. mural, moral, vocal, floral, local; 2. mural, moral, coral, pedal, medal; 3. final, spiral, vocal, focal, local, floral; 4. morality, legality, locality; 5. voice, vocalist, vocal

List 17: 1. normal, rival, total, scandal, loyal, royal; 2. normal, vital, hospital; 3. mental, formal, total, mortal, normal; 4. immortal, disloyal, informal; 5. formality, royalty, vitality, loyalty, mortality

List 18: 1. fossil, peril, repel, rebel; 2. pupil, pupil; 3. rebelled, rebelling, fulfilled, fulfilling; 4. pastel, tassel, tinsel, nostril, lapel; 5. fossil, devil, easel, chapel, hotel, nostril, pencil

List 19: 1. jewel, travel, carol, kernel, model, idol; 2. kernel, colonel; idle, idol; 3. novel, marvel, swivel, revel, hovel, patrol; 4. swivelled, controlling, patrolled, levelling, marvelled, travelling

List 20: 1. special, initial, crucial, official, spatial; 2. partial, official, material, trivial, social, essential; 3. serial, cereal; 4. immaterial, unofficial, inessential; 5. spatial, jovial, menial, genial, trivial, crucial

List 21: 1. property, liberty, cavity, vanity, poverty; 2. poverty, gravity, sanity, vanity, envy; 3. liberty, empty, property, envy, sanity, purity; 4. gravity, gravity; 5. family, familiar, familiarity, familiarize

List 22: 1. delay, annoy, dismay, array, destroy; 2. hooray, enjoy, employ, essay, allay, betray; 3. betray, convoy, astray, deploy, allay, array; 4. employment, enjoyment, portrayal, betrayal, deployment

List 23: 1. bizarre, bazaar; frieze, freeze; 2. bronze, zero, zebra, hazel, trapeze, zigzag, blazer, index; 3. relaxed, frenzied, snoozing, dizzying; 4. index, hazel, vex, blazer, frenzy, flux

List 24: 1. cue, queue; 2. quarries, quantities; qualifies; 3. question, query, enquire; 4. quiver, quibble, quarry, quarrel, queue, quirk, equal; 5. quarry, queasy, query, quartet, quiver, quibble, quirk

List 25: 1. squander, conquer, squirm, squad, squat; 2. squatting, squeezing, squealing; 3. squid, squire, squirrel, square, liquid; 4. squash, squash; 5. squirt, squeal, squabble, squirm, square, squat, squire

List 26: 1. whet, wet, wine, white; 2. whence, wheat, whine, whimsy, whirl; 3. whiff, whilst, whine, whirl, whisker, whittle; 4. whinny, whittle, whimsy, wheedle, whack, whimper, whence

List 27: 1. emphasising, emphatic, emphatically; 2. triumph, graph, physical, emphasis, phrase, sphere, trophy; 3. phase, faze; 4. sphinx, pharaoh, phone, physical; 5. orphan, sphinx, phantom, phoenix, pharaoh, physics

List 28: 1. knock, listen, knead, fasten; 2. moistened, moistening, hastened, hastening, fastened, fastening; 3. need, knead; knot, not; knit, nit; 4. knee, kneel, knelt; 5. faster, fastest, fastener

List 29: 1. climb, comb, answer, doubt; 2. crumb, yacht, sign, thumb; 3. stalk, stalk, stork; 4. sign, yacht, answer, column, stalk; 5. debt, yacht, doubt, comb, limb, sign

List 30: 1. bright, height, night; 2. sight, site; write, right; night, knight; 3. high, night, right, bright, tight, light, sight; 4. might, might; right, right; light, light

List 31: 1. nought, ought, enough, bough, sought, tough, fought; 2. bought; brought; 3. bough, bow; fought, fort; sought, sort, ruff, rough; threw, through; 4. cough, drought, through

List 32: 1. wreath, wrangle, wrath, wrench, wring, wreck; 2. write, wrote, written; 3. wrinkle, wrangle, wriggle; 4. ring, wring; rung, wrung; wrote, rote; wretch, retch; rap, wrap

List 33: 1. glove, company, monk, flood, money, month, blood; 2. front, monk, dozen, oven; 3. above, front, monk: 4. money, lovely, front, company, comfort; 5. moneyed, honeyed, monkeyed

List 34: 1. wander, water, wash, wad, warn; 2. ward, wan, waft, thwart, wad, waltz; 3. war, wore; worn, warn; 4. watched, watchful, unwatchable; 5. watch, watch; ward, ward

List 35: 1. worse, worm, worry, swap, work; 2. swapped, swapping, swatted, swatting; 3. woman, swarm, worm, women, swan, word, swat; 4. wonder, wander; worst, wurst; worse, worst

List 36: 1. drowsy, rowdy, power; 2. flour, flower; 3. dowdy, downy, dowry, cower, prowess, trowel, bower; 4. powder, shower, meow, vowel, dowry, tower; 5. rowdier, rowdiest, dowdier, dowdiest

List 37: 1. endow, mildew, wallow, askew, bestow; 2. cashew, elbow, shadow, widow, meadow, nephew; 3. swallow, swallow; window, window; 4. guffaw, askew, wallow, bungalow, bestow, mildew, curfew

List 38: 1. portrait, detail, daily, daisy; 2. diary, dairy; 3. fairy, fountain, mountain, curtain, mermaid, dairy, daisy; 4. repair, portrait, daily, maintain, despair, fountain; 5. entertaining, entertainer, entertainment

List 39: 1. season, eager, reason, weather, dreary, leather; 2. steamer, treason, beacon, heather, beaker, dreary, eager; 3. season, season; 4. wearily, weariness, drearily, dreariness; 5. whether, whether, weather

List 40: 1. reprieve, believe, courier, retrieve, glacier; 2. soldier, pierce, mischief, grieve, fierce, frontier, reprieve; 3. belief, believe, believable; 4. soldier (die), (lie) beliefs; 5. achieving, achievable, retrieving, retrievable, mischievous

List 41: 1. feign, conceit, weir, sovereign, conceive, perceive; 2. heir, seize, conceit, weird; 3. deceive, perceive, conception, reception; 4. air, heir; seize, seas; rein, reign; vein, vain

List 42: 1. cruise, crews; brews, bruise; suite, sweet; guilt, gilt; 2. guilt, suit, fruit, juice, circuit; 3. suit, suit; 4. pursuit, suite, circuit, recruit, guile, guise, guild

List 43: 1. adhere, adopt, amend, advise, abroad, amuse; 2. adopt, admit, award, adjust, abroad; 3. advice, advise, advice; 4. adjustment, advancement, amusement; 5. admit, adhere, aware, adore, advise

List 44: 1. compel, concept, confess, conduct, concern, conceal; 2. confusion, confession, conclusion; 3. confide, compel, confirm, compare, combine; 4. conclude, confuse, concern, concept, compare; 5. conviction, conception, confirmation

List 45: 1. defer, deduct, disgust, dispute, deliver; 2. defeat, depose, dispute, declare, devote; 3. discussion, devotion, deduction, declaration; 4. define, defer, devote, depose, disgust, dismiss; 5. discussed, disgust

List 46: 1. insist, excuse, inform, instruct, excel; 2. expression, exception, instruction, inversion, inclusion; 3. import, include, inform; 4. excite, impose, inverse, except, exceed, instruct; 5. accept, except, accept

Complete Graded Spelling Lists with Spelling and Vocabulary Exercises

Year Four, cont/...

List 47: 1. prevail, promote, prelude, profess, provoke; 2. presents, presence; 3. prevail, provoke, profess, prelude, pervade, proclaim; 4. prediction, promotion, precision, preparation, proclamation; 5. predict, prelude, prepare, preview

List 48: 1. repent, recoil, refine, remote, recite, restrain; 2. refuse, refuse; 3. restrain, remote, repeat, recite, record; 4. reveal, recite, recoil, remind, report; 5. repeat, reveal, reduce, recite

List 49: 1. forth, fourth; 2. primary, primarily, primitive, primate; 3. Friday, Monday, Saturday, Thursday, Tuesday, Wednesday; 4. first, second, third, fourth, fifth, eighth; 5. second, second; primary, primary

List 50: 1. evening, morning, summer, winter, autumn, spring, (month of your birthday); 2. spring, spring; 3. autumn, evening, winter; November, August, December; 4. morning, mourning; 5. May, morning, June, July, summer

Complete Graded Spelling Lists with Spelling and Vocabulary Exercises

MY RESULTS

Year Three

Mark (out of 22)

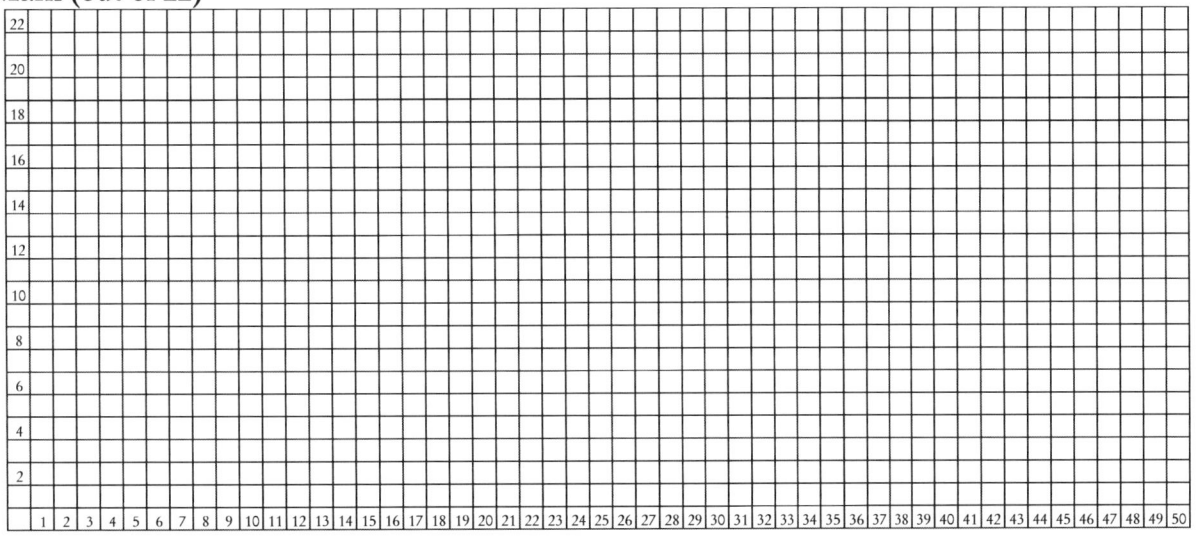

Test

Year Four

Mark (out of 22)

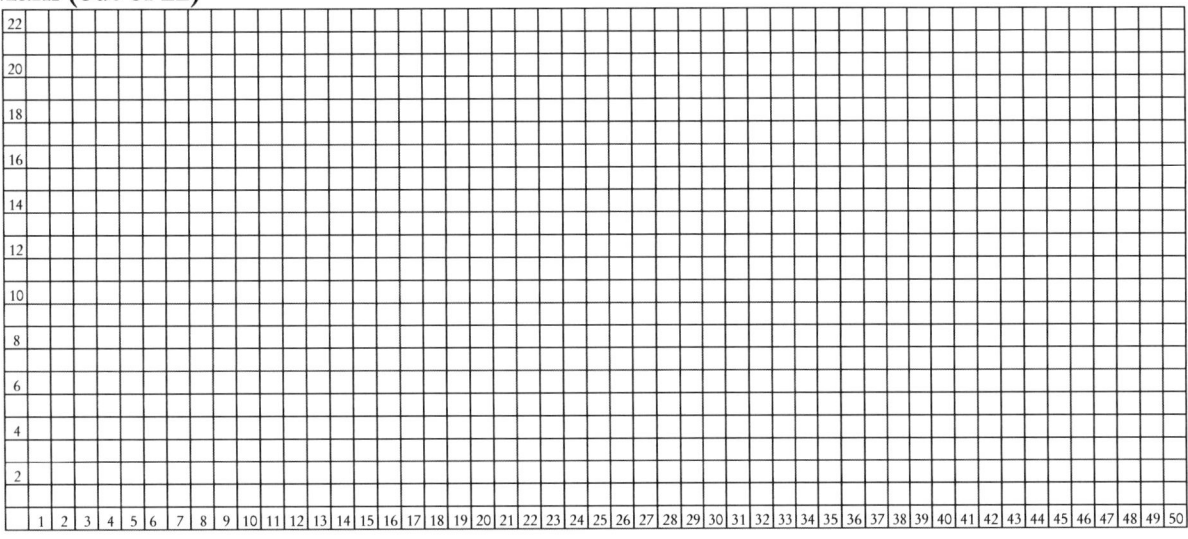

Test

Printed in Great Britain
by Amazon